I0762201

WELL SAID WELL READ

WELL SAID WELL READ

SELECTED TRUE STORIES FROM THE FIRST DECADE OF WRITERS READ

EDITED BY **EDWARD McCANN**

Writers Read Press
New York

1 WRITER. 5 MINUTES. 650 WORDS.

writersREAD

ISBN 978-1-7343808-6-6
writersread.org

For Ricki

"The most powerful words in English are 'Tell me a story,' words that are intimately related to the complexity of history, the origins of language, the continuity of the species, the taproot of our humanity, our singularity, and art itself."

—Pat Conroy

Welcome

It seems that we human beings have been sitting around in circles—caves, campfires, amphitheaters, basements, nursery schools—telling stories to one another since our first ancestors unlocked language hidden in their souls. It's what we do. It's who we are. It's how we remind ourselves of our shared humanity.

After ten years spent reviewing and editing thousands of stories at *Writers Read*, I have learned a few things about storytelling. First off, all stories are not created equal. Some stories are little more than kindly—or sometimes not so kindly—kinds of gossip, real or imagined, true or false, that we tell one another as distractions or entertainments around the proverbial water cooler at work . . . or shoulder to shoulder to shoulder at some local watering hole . . . or packed in a car driving around town with no particular place to go. Those stories may be funny or sad or ironic or salacious or frightening, but they don't—and they won't—transport anyone around the human circle into the sacred realm that connects us to one another.

But then there are the kind of stories that bring us into each other's embrace—tales that shine a light on our shared experience of life on earth in all its joys, impediments, and sorrows. A remarkable aspect of those stories, as Joseph Conrad told us in Heart of Darkness, is how "the meaning of an episode [is] not inside like a kernel but outside, enveloping the tale which brought it out only as a glow brings out a haze." Each of those deeply personal narratives serves as a vehicle to bring a reader or a listener into what I'm calling the real story, the subtextual story, a magical combination of words that can carry us wordlessly, one by one, toward a more far-reaching understanding of who we are—and, just as important, who we are to each other.

And so it is with the sixty-two stories in this remarkable anthology that Ed McCann has assembled to celebrate ten years of *Writers Read* spreading the good word. Each story is magical. Each an incantation. Out of the cacophonous wilderness, a sharp and clear truth-telling voice letting us know we are not alone.

—Steve Lewis, *Writers Read* Senior Editor

Contents

Lynn Ahrens

Lynn Ahrens was born a lyricist, setting her own words to the tune of "Frosty the Snowman" at age three and a half. In her first job out of college—secretary in a New York advertising agency—she spent her lunch hours playing guitar and writing songs. Soon thereafter she became a mainstay singer/songwriter for the famed animated series *Schoolhouse Rock.* Lynn has gone on to great acclaim with her extensive work in theater, film, and television. Her projects include such gems as the Broadway musicals *Ragtime, Anastasia, Seussical,* and *Once on This Island.* Lynn has been consistently honored for her work, earning Tony, Emmy, and Olivier Awards as well as nominations for two Oscars and four Grammys and an induction into the Theater Hall of Fame. She's also published many short stories and essays, but her heart always returns to rhyme.

Going Hollywood

Lynn Ahrens

Adapted from "Going Hollywood," first published in Narrative magazine.

February 10, 1998. I'm in the shower when the phone rings. A minute later my husband hands the receiver through the shower door.

"Hi," a woman says. "I'm from the *Asbury Park Press*. Have you heard? You've been nominated for two Academy Awards—Best Song and Best Score."

I scream, grab a towel, kiss my husband, and race to call my mother.

"How wonderful!" she cries. "It's an honor just to be nominated!"

And there it is—the tiny "pinprick in the bubble of joy"—my mother's special way of protecting me from life's inevitable disappointments.

You see, I'm the lyricist for Twentieth Century Fox's animated feature film *Anastasia*, and we're up against one of the biggest movies of all time, James Cameron's *Titanic*. Our nominated song, "Journey to the Past," will compete with "My Heart Will Go On," sung by Celine Dion. And even my mother knows—we're going to lose.

I'm a pants-and-baggy-sweaters kind of girl, clothes that hide everything. But now I'm going to the Oscars, and my phone is ringing off the hook: What are you going to wear? Friends assure me that designers will come flocking with outfits and jewelry. But the film's press rep explains, "Sorry, dear. No one's ever heard of you."

Off I trudge to Bloomingdale's, Bendel, Bergdorf, bargain basements, and bridal boutiques, where mirrors make clear—I must never be allowed to wear a long gown. But at last I find something to love—a champagne lace blazer, exquisitely embroidered all over with tiny crystals, and matching satin pants. The outfit is obscenely expensive, but it's marked half price, and I also find gorgeous shoes on sale, like magical glass slippers. From head to toe, I'm a vision in nonrefundable glamour.

At home, I try on my Oscar outfit again and slowly realize why the price was reduced. The crystals embroidered along the arms of the blazer snag on the lace. If I let my arms touch my sides, they stick there and must be torn away with brute force, leaving tiny tatters. If I hug someone wearing lace, we'll stick together like Velcro sausages. I realize I'll have to walk the red carpet with my arms held out like a ballerina in first position.

In Los Angeles, Oscar festivities abound. At the nominees' luncheon, we're assembled on a stage and called one by one to receive certificates. For some reason, they've decided to call us in reverse alphabetical order. David Zippel is first and heads off to work the room. I'm last. Helena Bonham Carter is just before me and leaves with a look of pity. By the time I'm freed, the food is gone and so are the guests. Can the red carpet be far behind?

Let me say, the red carpet isn't a long runner, as I'd imagined, but more like a bullring. We're sent into this screaming arena to do press together with fifteen-year-old Olympic champion Tara Lipinski, who skated to gold with our nominated song.

"Make sure to stay with Tara," the press agent whispers. "No one's ever heard of you."

That evening, the Shrine Auditorium is packed, and excitement is high. My magical glass slippers completely fog up in anticipation.

When the Best Song category is finally announced, Madonna calls the nominees' names. She pronounces mine incorrectly—"Lynn A-herns." And now, she opens the envelope, and says in a monotone, "Oh, what a shocker." Celine Dion rises, straight and slim as an Oscar statuette. And my shoes instantly defog.

But the night is filled with parties and promise. Elton John is at Spago. Lights glitter like the crystals on my beautiful jacket. The air is velvet. Twentieth Century Fox has given us a limo and driver. I'm the youngest and the best-dressed I'll ever be again.

I hear my mother's voice, soft and sweet. "It's an honor just to be nominated." And it is. Off we fly through the mysterious Los Angeles streets, wrapped in our own personal bubble of joy.

Arthur Bell

Art Bell is a writer and former television executive known for developing and launching the Comedy Channel (later Comedy Central) while at HBO and, as president of Court TV, overseeing daily live courtroom coverage and the production of hundreds of hours of original true-crime television series, documentaries, and movies. His memoir, *Constant Comedy: How I Started Comedy Central and Lost My Sense of Humor*, was a finalist in the 2020 Best Book Awards. Art has had short stories, nonfiction, and satire published in several journals, including *Lowestoft Chronicle, Aethlon: The Journal of Sports Literature, The Ocotillo Review, Fiction Southeast, High Shelf Press,* and *Writers Read. What She's Hiding*, his first novel, was published in March 2025.

A Few Minor Alterations

Arthur Bell

I started trumpet lessons in fifth grade; by high school, I was good enough to play in the marching band.

Our first band rehearsal was on the football field under a blazing late-August sun. There were fifty-four of us, all in sweat-soaked shorts and T-shirts, all hot and tired before we even started. I held a soggy mimeographed sheet diagramming where my "squad" of four trumpeters would march so that the band spelled out LHS (for Lakewood High School) in giant human letters as we played the school fight song, "On for Lakewood." By late afternoon, we were overheated and sunburned crimson. I thought we'd never get it right, but finally everything clicked into place, and after the band formed those giant letters on the field, we were allowed to go home.

We got our band uniforms when school started a week later. The jacket and pants were deep blue trimmed in white, our school colors. There were white leather spats that buckled over shoes, and striped suspenders that crossed in back. And, to top it off, a foot-high furry blue hat with a chinstrap. It looked like the Bride of Frankenstein's hairdo, dyed velvety blue. I hoped the hat might make me look taller, and I needed all the help I could get since I was the shortest kid in the freshman class.

Because I was so short, I worried that the uniform might not fit. As soon as Mr. Unger, our band director, handed it to me, I fished around inside the jacket to check the size: XXS, the smallest high school band uniform made. I took the uniform, hat, spats, and suspenders home, ran upstairs to the privacy of my bedroom, and put everything on. The pants were so big that I could hold the waist six inches from my body. I looked at myself in the mirror; the jacket seemed to swallow me whole, and the sleeves hung down to my knees. With the suspenders and spats, it looked like I was wearing a clown suit. The only thing missing was the big red nose.

It was a week before the first game, enough time to make alterations, but my mother didn't sew, and I was too embarrassed to ask anyone else to do it. I found a box of safety pins and began the process of pulling, folding, and pinning the uniform into a wearable size. I shortened the pants and sleeves, and I pulled in the waist so that it could be belted without bagging. When I finished, I climbed into the uniform, careful to avoid all the safety pins holding the excess fabric in check, and stood at the mirror. The pants and sleeves were the right length, but the jacket drooped and draped as if it hung on a tiny clothes hanger. The pants crotch hung well below my actual crotch, and the zipper fly looked about two feet long. I swallowed hard and turned away from the mirror, knowing there was nothing more I could do.

On game day, my father drove me, uniformed and holding my fuzzy blue hat, in silence to the high school. "See if you can get a ride home," he said as I climbed out of the car, struggling with all that pinned excess yardage. Walking down the hall to the band room, my pants broadcast a swish, swish sound, and I braced myself for withering looks and cruel laughter.

But when I walked into the band room, no one seemed to care that I looked like Bozo the Trumpeter. A few people said hi to me as we all got our music and instruments ready. Even though I felt like the sour note in the opening chord, I began to relax, and to think that maybe I belonged. Even though the uniform didn't fit—I fit in.

Elva Bennett

Elva Bennett is an artist, teacher, climate scientist, and sometimes writer. They lived most of their years in North Carolina, sweating, eating grits, and trying to move north. They now live and work in Seattle, Washington, where they are well-suited the moody weather and proximity to water. Their art, like their early writing, observes queerness, connection, and change.

A Table in the Sun

Elva Bennett

Godfathers is a loose and largely inaccurate description for two men—a couple, as it turns out—whom I've known all my life. I use it for lack of a better word: They're not technically related, but far closer than any aunt, uncle, or grandparent could be—and supremely hip to all the family gossip. I once confessed my misnomer to them as they chauffeured me around New England on college visits.

"Then how about *fairy godfathers*?" Ed had joked at the time.

Richard and Ed are family friends who have been close with my mother and grandparents since Mom was a little girl. As a child, they showered me with love and attention, sent me letters on holidays, and brought me books during their annual visits. When they came into town, they came together. When they left, they left together. I never knew life without them, and I thought of them as nothing more or less than loving family members whom I couldn't wait to see again.

My realization came the summer I was thirteen years old. Richard and Ed were staying with us, and everyone was sitting on the back patio of my family home—Mom, Dad, Richard, and Ed at the patio table with the big umbrella shielding them from the summer sun, me a few feet away on the shady back porch steps with my arms around the family dog. I looked at the four of them, their chairs arranged so that my parents and our guests were mirrored across the table, and, for no particular reason, I recognized I was staring at two couples. Oh my God! Richard and Ed were gay!

I'd heard about these gay people, and, suddenly, here they were sitting in my backyard and part of my family.

I sat there on the steps stunned into silence, as if I had just uncovered a deep family secret. I grew up in a home with good politics and common human decency, which is to say that my silence wasn't judgment or foreboding, but a mental pause to categorize the previously uncategorized, put a new label on people whose labels I thought I knew, insert an otherness.

Maybe it was the problematic vernacular I heard flying around my middle school or my crossing of the age threshold to be included in discussions of politics at the dinner table, or maybe it was all those *Will & Grace* reruns, but somehow my heteronormative worldview had cracked open just wide enough for me to comprehend that this pair of almost-relatives were in just as much of a romantic relationship as my aunts and uncles, grandmas and grandpas, Mom and Dad.

Even then I felt stupid for not realizing sooner. I tried to nonchalantly mention this newfound fact to my mom a few days later.

"Richard and Ed are gay."

Both a statement and a question. She furrowed her eyebrows, amused, before confirming, as if to say, *Duh kid, water is wet*. My cover was blown.

After the rush of surprise came intense joy and relief. It was as if I experienced the excitement of a new relationship and the satisfaction of witnessing years of happiness all in an instant. My fairy godfathers were in love and happy and would be, always.

Eventually, I joined them at the table in the sun, approaching slowly and acting normal so no one might suspect my recent discovery. I watched Richard and Ed closely for the rest of the visit. They worked so seamlessly in tandem and gravitated around one another with the ease and stability of planets. Nothing new, but now obviously meaningful.
My understanding of their connection did not shift, the constellation of loving relationships I aspired to merely grew. How odd it was to assign a word to something that I'd always known.

Jamie Bernstein

Jamie Bernstein is an author, broadcaster, filmmaker, and concert narrator. In addition to writing her many articles and concert narrations, Jamie travels extensively, speaking about music as well as about her father, composer and conductor Leonard Bernstein. Jamie's film documentary, *Crescendo! The Power of Music*, has won numerous prizes and is now viewable on iTunes. Jamie's memoir, *Famous Father Girl*, was published by HarperCollins. You can learn more about Jamie's multifaceted life on her website: jamiebernstein.net.

Gratis

Jamie Bernstein

By my mid-sixties, I'd journeyed along the familiar human landscape of ups and downs: marriage, death of parents, childbirth (twice), breast cancer (twice), divorce, professional failures and successes, all the many mile-markers.

There are advantages to reaching this age: for example, to have ceased being an erotic object to men. No more lascivious glances, wolf whistles, or subway feel-ups. There is power in knowing you can make yourself invisible in public: just some generic, diminutive, middle-aged woman, darting along in her dark colors. Smoke-gray ninja.

Occasionally I've mused that another romantic relationship might possibly still be out there waiting for me. I have curiosity and energy; I can pull myself together, look good enough—even if it does take, as my friends are tired of hearing me say, twice the effort for half the results.

But in the next breath I'd wonder: How would I feel about putting this irreversibly disintegrating body back in action? And would I even remember how stuff worked? Maybe I'm better off with the morning snuggles of my dog—who, in almost all respects, is the best bed companion I've ever had.

On holidays, my extended family—and all our dogs—nestle together in the old place in Connecticut. Thanksgiving is our favorite: no religion, no presents, just close kin, lots of food, and all the heartfelt thank-yous.

Next best is Passover—the Jewish Thanksgiving—featuring more family, feasting, and thanks (albeit tinged with those problematic assertions about being "the chosen people"). Everyone's favorite Seder song is "Dayenu"—translated as "it would have been enough." An excerpt:

> If He had split the sea for us, and had not taken us through it on dry land—*Dayenu*!
>
> If He had taken us through the sea on dry land, and had not drowned our oppressors in it—*Dayenu*!

And so on, for many verses, none of which we could ever properly reproduce in Hebrew—but oh, how heartily we chimed in on the catchy "Da, da, ye-nu, Da, da, ye-nu!" chorus.

My life has been very full lately: at least a hundred "Dayenu" verses of more-than-enough. So I don't ask for additional goodies; I lean toward thank you, not please, in my prayers. (Anyway, I don't subscribe to begging a deity for favors.)

Then the unexpected, unprayed-for thing happened. A person came back into my life, a person from forty-one years ago. Once this thunderbolt of reconnection was upon me, it seemed inevitable, essential. And I *did* remember how stuff worked. My body (my rickety old body!) had found its completing piece—like the two rocks I once found on the beach that seamlessly conjoined when I slid their irregular surfaces against each other in just a certain way.

There's a pure, present-tense rigor to gratitude. It requires discipline; it's a practice. The trick for me, now, is to embrace this new embarrassment of riches, to repel the toxic shadow of "Do I deserve this?" (That shadow can shut a heart right down.) I'll try to keep out of my own way: accept what fell to earth and landed in my lap, unasked for. Unpaid for. *Gratis*.

When we're suffused in the goodness of life, we have the overwhelming urge to thank *somebody*. Yet I don't really believe that some discrete entity is arranging my circumstances. I sense it more as the universe wheeling around—for no reason, or reasons far beyond my understanding—and depositing me, for a while at least, in the light-drenched place where I am now.

Mary Catherine Bolster

Mary Catherine Bolster grew up in Iowa but not on a farm. She has been writing in one form or another since her first feature column in *The Compass*, her high school paper. With advanced degrees in nursing and medical ethics, she began her career on the clinical faculty of the University of Iowa; she has published articles in *The Linacre Quarterly* and other medical/ethical journals as well as consumer-oriented articles for regional magazines and national trade publications. Her position as national director of marketing and education for a healthcare organization led to her founding MCB Communications; her company served healthcare and not-for-profit clients, specializing in capital campaigns, consumer and medical writing, and public relations. Though she lives in Manhattan, from time to time she yearns for her beloved prairie.

B-Flat

Mary Catherine Bolster

Growing up in 1950s Iowa, my sister Beverly, seven years older, was my de facto mother. It was Beverly who sustained me through childhood tragedies like my beloved parakeet's death when I was seven. Took the sting out of a grade school bully's cruel words. Taught me how to make doll clothes from pastel flannel and satin ribbons while sitting on her big double bed.

And when I mastered playing piano, we made music together. I would accompany her strong soprano voice: opera arias, Broadway tunes, church hymns.

After she married and moved to Cedar Rapids, I married too, but I didn't stay in Iowa. I moved a thousand miles away to Philadelphia.

Time, careers, petty jealousies, and foolish misunderstandings eventually replaced our harmonies with silence. I watched from a distance as sips of wine became her solace against the discordance of everyday life.

Eventually Beverly stopped singing. Not in a church choir. Or a local a cappella group. Nothing.

And then—the dementia.

My sister died last year. Beverly was seventy-five.

On the subway platform, the B train rolls to a stop at Eighty-First

Street. I step into the crowded, hot car. I'm overdressed, can't move my arms to loosen my wool scarf. No earbuds to create a music bubble. No cell service to check HopStop. Can't see the transit map and can't move anyway amidst this throng of no-eye-contact, stone-faced New Yorkers.

Why this journey? To see a vocal coach, of all things. My new shrink, whom I sought out in a last-ditch attempt to find out why I'm still so angry with my dear departed sister, said: "Performing makes you feel heard. Connected. So *do* it."

I found Jean through the Open Center catalog. Sixty-ish, thin as a rail, graceful, articulate, classically trained. She thinks I've got talent—should begin auditioning again. *Really Jean. I'm almost seventy.*

For half the lesson she softens my rigid body using precise Alexander Technique cues, her fingertips barely touching my torso, my diaphragm freer with each breath. After a warm-up, I sing Sondheim or Jerry Herman or eighteenth-century solos in Italian. Somehow my voice seems clearer, lighter. I'm lighter. For that one hour each week, there's nothing in the world but music. Something to purge this anger.

After the session, I rush out to get to the Fulton Street station with five minutes to spare. Above the hum of the morning commute, I hear what sounds like organ and harp music coming from the terminal lobby. I walk up just as a lone violinist begins to play Gounod's "Ave Maria."

My sister and I loved this piece of music, this gem, a masterful combination of a much-loved Bach prelude and the soulful melody Gounod added years later. It was always a crowd-pleaser when we performed it for family gatherings, or local weddings, or High Mass at St. Joseph's.

I lean against a steel pillar in the morning light to listen and remember a summer day when we were performing this piece in a clapboard country church, shutters opened to the surrounding green fields. Beverly's voice perfectly suited for the melody's range, filling every corner.

I stay there, transported, slipping on my Ray-Bans to conceal the tears. I am the sole audience for this pop-up performance.

My train comes and goes. But I do not walk away, I cannot. Not until the violinist plays the last, luxurious B-flat.

Colin Broderick

Colin Broderick was raised Irish Catholic in the heart of Northern Ireland. In 1988, at the age of twenty, he moved to the Bronx to drink, work construction, and pursue his dream of becoming a writer. For the next twenty years, as he drank himself into oblivion: there were failed marriages, car wrecks, hospitals, and jail cells. Few people who have been a slave to an addiction as vicious, destructive, and unrelenting as Colin's have lived to tell their tale. His memoir, *Orangutan*, is the story of an Irish drunk unlike any you've met before. Colin has written a play, *Father Who*, and published articles in *The Irish Echo, The Irish Voice,* and *The New York Times.*

An Irish Writer in New York

Colin Broderick

In 1988, the New York I arrived in was one of abandoned buildings, battered window shades, and blackened shells along the highway. Uptown was boom box, squeegee men, and sneaker wars. Down on The Deuce they were shilling sleaze and switchblades for as cheap as a buck. Pickpockets, peddlers, and preachers stood shoulder to shoulder with ruddy-faced Irish American cops too outnumbered and sweaty to give a goddamn. Back then, Forty-Second Street was a scabbed vein, so pockmarked and contaminated it was practically its own ecosystem.

Downtown was squatters' rights, artists, and dope dealers alongside old-school Eastern European grandmothers in headscarves lugging shopping bags up Second Avenue. Streetwalkers bold as peacocks preened themselves on the cobblestoned streets of the West Village while over around Saint Mark's, pale-faced boys in skinny pants and Mohawks graffitied shuttered tenement walls and nodded out in Tompkins Square Park. New York was a city of shadows and ghosts and blocks you didn't dare venture down alone.

It was a town that felt lived in. A town with an active working class. Madness and danger were a staple of everyday life.

Not that it was easy; it was a hustle. It was a dodge and a weave, blindfolded and drunk, through a minefield. Each new step possibly your last. But man was it alive: an urban landscape so rich in story that words practically rained down off the fire escapes like rust chips and danced their way into my soul in ready-made paragraphs.

Being young and Irish in New York, I was bequeathed the added romance of a literary heritage, even if I didn't understand it fully back then.

New York is where Irish literature comes to get its passport stamped.

As a young writer I had a dream that one day I would see my name on the spine of a book, on a shelf, wedged next to Banville and Behan.

There was only one small catch: I couldn't write.

I could drink though. Boy could I drink!

So I drank . . . I worked construction, fell in and out of love—and marriages—like a man possessed.

In the summer of 2006 I was thirty-eight years old, living in a fifth-floor walk-up in Hell's Kitchen. I weighed 115 pounds. I was unemployable. I was somehow surviving on a diet of beer, vodka, weed, and cocaine. In my alcoholic madness I had been stabbed, beaten, jailed, and hospitalized. The idea of taking a swan dive off my fifth-floor balcony onto Ninth Avenue had begun to haunt me as a viable alternative to the chorus of demons that plagued my every waking thought.

One night, lying in the dark alone, sipping on whiskey, listening to the blare of traffic below my window, I finally understood that this was the place right before death. If something didn't change soon, they would find me here on the floor of this apartment surrounded by empty bottles. This was the end. It had to be. I moved to a friend's farmhouse upstate and began to write like my life depended upon it. It did.

Within a year I'd sold my drinking memoir Orangutan to Random House.

Over eleven years without a drink, I published three books, directed two of my own plays, saw my name in *The New Yorker* and *The New York Times*, took the stage at Lincoln Center to read my own work. I wrote and directed two feature movies. I met my wife, and I became a father to a girl and then a boy. I am not rich. I am not a household-name author. But I am still writing. In my own roundabout way, I wound up living the very life that I'd always dreamed might be possible. I am an Irish writer in New York.

Zach Buckner

Zach Buckner is a copywriter and humor writer splitting his time between Brooklyn and Barryville, New York. If he didn't have to make money to live, he'd spend his time walking. Everywhere. Between boroughs, state lines—over oceans if he could. On his walks, he'd scour the land for dumplings that would blow his proverbial mind. He'd also pet every stray cat he encountered and buy them a can of wet food before they went on their separate paths. He's the middle child of five and cried during his bar mitzvah when his rabbi said he suffered from a classic case of "middle child syndrome." He grew up in northern Westchester—*not* southern Westchester.

Shalom to All That

Zach Buckner

Every morning I wake with a tinge of disappointment. I'm not saying my life is a disappointment or I'm jumping off the Goethals between meetings or anything like that. But every morning, for thirty-two years, I've woken with disappointment over my body. When I was sixteen, I'd stare at my protruding stomach, the sweat already starting at 7 a.m., and my dirty-blond, Jewish curls. I did the same at twenty-one. And twenty-five. And twenty-eight. You get the picture.

I didn't think I could shave away my Jewishness and my insecurities by buzzing my curly locks. But I didn't not think it either. The decision came to me after being mistaken for Abraham on Fordham's campus. Who's Abraham? I have no idea. When I asked the student, she just said, "He looks like you." Stammering, schvitzing, a little paunchy? Abraham seemed great.

Shortly after the Abraham incident, I was like Moses and parted the curls of my hair and shaved my head. "But your hair is your thing," my friend said, with a buzzer humming in one hand and a PBR in the other. With each buzz, a piece of me floated away. *Buzz*—goodbye, complicated relationships with food and toilet paper ply! *Buzz*—sayonara, my mother's fear of choking on burgers, balloons, and saliva. *Buzz*—shalom to all of that.

When my friend finished, I barely recognized myself. First, I didn't know that I had bumps on my head. Instinctively, I called my mom, and before I could get a word out, she asked, "What's wrong?" Now we were both terrified of the bumps. Our shared Jewish panic told us that, sure, on the one hand it could be the natural shape of my skull. But far more likely, it was a malignant tumor that had spread to three different parts of my brain.

Second, I couldn't tell if I was balding or not. Was my hairline always pushed back? They say your hairline can be linked to your maternal grandfather. Since I'd already informed my mom that she'd have one fewer son in the very near future, I decided to ask my aunt about my grandfather's hairline.

"What's it matter if he was bald? He owned a business," my aunt said. "He was a good man. Depressed, sure. Always disappointed too. Anyways, you shouldn't be worried about losing your hair, you should be worried about getting diabetes. That's what killed him. Not a widow's peak. He made your grandmother a widow."

Third, I had a serious glower on my face. Gone was the open-armed invitation to kvetch about bowel troubles, good meals, or the minor annoyances fueling our days. Instead, I looked like I wanted to talk about lawn maintenance or golden retrievers.

Over the next few years, I lived by the Garfunkel principle. Did I look like I could be a stand-in for Art Garfunkel? If so, Parsley, Sage, Rosemary, and Thyme for a buzz.

It wasn't until later that I realized my hair was the only thing I truly loved about myself. After a lifetime of body hatred, my hair stood out on a body that wanted to fade in. My hair became a blanket I wanted to either wrap around myself or throw in the fire, or, often, both at the same time. People envied, gushed, fawned over my hair. But when I tried to offer myself that same acceptance and love, I buzzed it away. I couldn't face my own face.

With each buzz, I thought I was staring the world down and shouting, "What do you think of me now?" I was really only shouting at myself, of course.

I woke up today without my morning disappointment. I've come to love my curls, my Jewishness, my body. Plus, my shaved head makes me look like a skinhead. Which doesn't feel on-brand for an Abraham or a Zach.

Cindy Clement Carlson

Cindy Clement Carlson is the mother of three kids, all raised in Sandy Hook, Connecticut. She was at work in the Sandy Hook Elementary School library media center—and her daughter was present—on the day of the December 2012 shooting. Cindy currently serves as director of communications and major giving at WMNR Fine Arts Radio, a classical music station in Connecticut. She's written widely about her experience at Sandy Hook Elementary School, with publications in *The Newtowner, Marie Claire, School Library Journal,* and *If I Don't Make It, I Love You: Survivors in the Aftermath of School Shootings.*

The Commitment to Findability

Cindy Clement Carlson

I am reading *The Library Book* by Susan Orlean. She describes a library's need for order and proper shelving, observing that "the commitment to findability is absolute." A mis-shelved book may as well be thrown into the trash. School librarians ask their students not to reshelve books they've browsed to avoid dolphin nonfiction in mythology, or panda books in the origami section.

After you've listened to gunshots kill twenty kids and six teachers, the library can help you get yourself back in order, too.

After the December 2012 shooting at Sandy Hook Elementary School, every book and magazine in the library media center was packed by professional library movers, trucked to a nearby mothballed school, and unpacked. Every Kindle, bookmark, and morning-meeting rug was taken from the sacred chaos of that building and brought to a former middle school in Monroe.

Over a wretched, extended winter break marked by funerals, our staff of three estimated how high an elementary student could reach on a middle school shelf. We evaluated our storage closet for its capacity to shelter students from gunfire. We unpacked familiar posters and signs, all while learning how to lock the doors quickly.

Then, the first day in Monroe for the students. Every aspect of school has changed, yet the library can remind you who you are. Remember how much you liked the stuffed dragon? It's still on top of the nonfiction shelf! Remember the bin of princess books? Yes, here it is! Sharks? Right here in Dewey 597.3!

Library cards, also brought to Monroe from Sandy Hook, were out on our new circulation desk, by the computer as always. You're a third grader, your card is still blue. There's the corner where the lamination has been picked each year since the card was earned as a kindergartener. And yes, hearing that metal water bottle clatter to the floor in the hall was terrifying; let's wheel the library cart around so we'll know what that sounds like.

Most satisfying was fulfilling a hold placed in the old school. With effortful handwriting, students had filled out hold slips in Sandy Hook to request books already checked out. When those books were returned to the new school, I silently thanked the upset parents who had the presence of mind to remember it was library day and enthusiastically informed students that their requests were in!

Never mind that the staff was accounting for books left in classrooms where the shooting had occurred, that we wrapped a rubber band around a stack of twenty library cards of students who had died, that we threw away overdue notices for students who had lost a sibling. For our young patrons we focused on what was consistent and still in place. Last night your mother explained how girls from your Brownie troop had died, but the next morning in the library, here are the Rookie Read-Abouts in the cart as always, square edges, lined up in Dewey order. Your bus stop has two fewer kids in the morning, but in the library, the tent card that shows your place at the table is propped up to greet you in January just like it did in December.

That first winter, MLK Day and Presidents' Day came quickly. Tucked in the back room for now were the books that described their death by shooting. But look! The Valentine books we've been displaying for years! Come check out *Clifford's First Valentine's Day* and *Fancy Nancy: Heart to Heart* just like you did when you were a second grader.

We strove to maintain our traditions. Caldecott Award Day! Nutmeg Novel Reveal Day! Six Caldecott Days later, we're still putting the pieces of ourselves back together as a town and a school community. I hope the library helped some of these kids find who they were before the shooting. The commitment to findability was absolute.

Ann Casapini

Ann Casapini is a yoga and meditation instructor who also loves to write, sing, and dance salsa. She has been published in *The Sun, Dunes Review,* and *Intima: A Journal of Narrative Medicine*. In addition, her work has been featured in various anthologies, including *Free Spirit, The Ocotillo Review, Fiction International, Barzakh, Crack the Spine, Still Point Arts Quarterly,* Medusa's Laugh Press, and Scablands Books. Ann is a regular contributor to both *Writers Read* and Military Experience & the Arts' online journal. Ann lives in Tuckahoe, New York, with her husband, son, and dog, Rocky.

Who's on First?

Ann Casapini

Over the course of a month, I sewed over five hundred tiny white pearls and sequins, one by one, onto my satin gown, and more onto my headpiece with a two-tiered veil.

I had searched bridal shops in Manhattan and Long Island for my gown, but none cost less than a thousand dollars. Then a friend told me about a place in Brooklyn thzat sold store samples. It was a huge showroom with hundreds of gowns lining the walls on tightly packed racks. After an hour of pulling down ho-hum dresses, my arms and shoulders were aching.

I was about to give up, but then I found "the one." It reminded me of a period costume from the late eighteenth century. It had an empire silhouette and a fitted bodice ending just below the bust, giving a high-waisted appearance. It had Juliet sleeves, long and tight with a puff at the top. The back was sheer lace with a line of twenty satin-covered buttons down the center. And the pièce de résistance was the cathedral train. The elongated back portion of the gown extending down to sweep onto the floor created a majestic look. I bought it for a hundred dollars.

All it needed were the pearls and sequins to catch light.

There were also vows to be written. David and I had decided to surprise each other on our wedding day. I knew his vows would be poetic and memorable; after all, he was a professional writer. Perhaps he would come up with something like the ending of *Ulysses*, when Molly Bloom finishes her passionate soliloquy with "yes I said yes I will Yes!"

So each night after my sewing sessions, I sat in the bathtub with pen and notebook, planning. *Write your vows. Wedding's almost here!* I scribbled and crossed out. Scribbled and crossed out.

To elevate my own three-page outpouring of hopes, dreams, and commitment, I chose Shakespeare's Sonnet 116, which begins, "Let me not to the marriage of true minds admit impediments."

And there were no impediments as I walked down the aisle of the Church of Our Savior on East Thirty-Eighth Street and Park Avenue. Everything was perfect. As I passed each pew, I could hear my guests gasp with awe at the elegance of my sparkling gown and the dramatic trail of my ruffle-edged train gliding across the marble floor.

The altar was surrounded by ornate bronze work and deep red gladiolas. I was to read my vows first. I had practiced it: five full minutes. And by the time I finished the sonnet, I could see my sister's eyes tear up with approval. Then, filled with anticipation to hear the vows my talented and romantic husband-to-be would offer me, I waited.

David coughed.

Coughed again.

Then paused before speaking: "As Yogi Berra once said: 'Baseball is the most important thing in the world, but love is pretty good, too.'"

My cheeks flushed.

He cleared his throat. Paused again. He'd never written out his vows! He was winging it! I was so stunned, I could hear nothing until he ended with: "And you can take that to the bank!" Done. Ninety seconds.

I wanted to bolt. But I was at the altar, with eighty-four pairs of eyes staring at me and my five hundred tiny white pearls and sequins. My feet would not move.

Holding me to my promise was the weight of my gown's twenty-foot train.

Jai Chakrabarti

Two-time O. Henry and Pushcart Prize winner **Jai Chakrabarti** is the author of the novel *A Play for the End of the World.* He was awarded the National Jewish Book Award for debut fiction and long listed for the PEN/Faulkner Award. Jai is also the author of the story collection *A Small Sacrifice for an Enormous Happiness*, which was among The *New Yorker*'s Best Books of 2023. His short fiction has been featured in *The Best American Short Stories, Ploughshares,* and *One Story* and performed for *Selected Shorts* at Symphony Space in New York City. Also published in *The Wall Street Journal, Fast Company, Writer's Digest, Berfrois*, and *LitHub,* he holds an MFA in creative writing from Brooklyn College. Born in Kolkata, India, he currently lives in New York with his family.

Giving Water

Jai Chakrabarti

Every year in the autumn my mother texts me to announce it's time to perform the *tarpan* ceremony. The text is precipitated by my father, who's most inclined to track when rituals of note fall on the calendar, but he's less inclined to partake in technology like texting. So, it's left to my mother to relay the Sanskrit mantras and for me to then recite the prayers and to give my ancestors water—in the morning, before I eat—so that no one in my long line will go thirsty.

I'm told I'm from a long line of philosophers, which continued with my parents but ended with me, the writer. I'm told my last name was an honorific given by a king as a sign of patronage. We come from a country that is still defined in many ways by castes, and my ancestors, the Brahmins, came not from royalty but from those who were well treated by the rich, a situation that in post-colonial India allowed them to flourish in the new world as lawyers, engineers, money makers.

Any religious sentiments I might have had have diminished with age, but in my birth country the far-right Hindutva groups have gained prominence. Emboldened by politicians in power, India has mainstreamed a version of Hinduism that lionizes its saints without interrogating the history of casteism and religious violence. In this country, through one lens, I'm seen as a minority, but in India my ancestors weren't the minority—at least, not in their influence—and I'm left to wrestle with their ghosts.

All of this came to the fore when my wife, Elana, was pregnant and we were discussing our future son's last name. Elana is Jewish, the granddaughter of Holocaust survivors, and it was important that her family name be preserved. My father was equally adamant that his grandson carry on the Chakrabarti line. This was vital for many reasons, he said, not the least of which had to do with water. In the *tarpan* ceremony, you're giving water to your ancestors. You name your grandparents, great grandparents, and as you ask for their blessing you make sure they're not thirsty in their afterlives. There's a sweetness to the ritual that reminds me of my boyhood on boats in the Ganges, the river imbued with holiness despite the traffic and the refuse and the stink, the sunset making the surface of the water shimmer as it must've for millennia.

Technically, this ritual can only be performed by those who bear their ancestors' last name. It's in the rules of the game, so to speak. Move on from your tribe in this way and you risk leaving your great grandparents parched.

But the love that Elana and I had found infused two cultures and religions. It was interfaith in the sense of that word that it was inside the faiths, allowing us to bring light from each of our traditions as we made our shared home. For both of us this meant embracing the truths that weren't so narrow. Logistically, this meant hyphenation. A child with a forever-long name.

When my mother learned what we'd decided, she tried to cajole us in every way. She said other students would laugh at our son's name, thinking it too long. But from attending middle school in America, I knew that it wasn't Elana's last name that would be a problem—hers is four letters—it would be mine. If his name were the subject of a playground taunt, it'd be because of my inheritance.

None of this stops me from dutifully giving water to my ancestors every year, though I know the tradition ends with me. Sometimes, I grieve the loss of this ritual, of the end of a line. Other times, I'm hopeful that whatever ritual my son may adopt, as one day he mourns me, will be wise and beautiful.

Barbara Chen

Barbara Chen was appointed by New York City Police Commissioner Raymond W. Kelly in 2006 as a special assistant and served as civilian director of media relations under the deputy commissioner for public information. She worked closely until 2014 with every NYPD bureau, from Community Affairs to Counterterrorism, covering major emergencies, including a car bomb in Times Square, Hurricane Sandy, civic unrest and crime, investigations, heroism, and the occasional animal rescue. Barbara was elected speaker of the 2011 class of Columbia Business School's Police Management Institute. She previously has worked for ABC News, Bloomberg Philanthropies, Columbia University, and UCLA's law school. Barbara is now a writer and media strategist for the Annenberg Foundation. She is originally from Torrance, California, and resides in Los Angeles.

Lights, Sirens, and Champagne

Barbara Chen

For seven years I drove a Chevrolet Impala, a hand-me-down with wide hips and windows as dark as my hair, so black a patrol car once pulled me over for illegal tint.

The police officer let me go because the Impala actually belonged to his employer and mine—the NYPD. The car was what the department calls "unmarked" and came with my job. I was a civilian special assistant in the NYPD press office, responding to catastrophes across the city at any hour of the day that news and laws could break. The car was my transport to emergencies and enabled me to staff officials in all five boroughs.

From the outside, the Impala could pass for any leftover on a used-car lot. But inside, a toggle switch unleashed deafening sirens and blinding police lights, including a detachable red lantern with a magnetic base so strong I had to arm wrestle the front dash to remove it.

The only thing subtle about the car was its paint—a metallic shade somewhere between the beach on an overcast day and smog. When prompted to note the car's color in the police mechanics' log, I decided to call it champagne.

"Champagne . . . ? That's a first," the mechanics chuckled. But then again, so was I. A petite Asian woman is not exactly who comes to mind when one thinks of law enforcement.

Like most people who live in New York, I had zero interest in driving or parking in the city. But the vehicle was nonnegotiable, so eventually Champagne and I flowed with traffic on the FDR Drive, from which I'd marvel at the cityscape before winding around the civic center labyrinth, waving to guards at familiar checkpoints. Driving their car, I got to know the police. Once, rushing to a Brooklyn hospital where a wounded officer was being treated, I tried taking a side street and nearly hit a plainclothes detective, recognizing too late the yellow tape behind him.

"Sorry!" I cried, presenting my department ID as he turned from startled to irritated. "I'm trying to get to Methodist. Do you know another way?"

"Not this way," he said. "This is the crime scene!"

As I reversed in an awkward three-point turn and receded into a line of unmoving cars, he hollered: "You got lights and sirens, honey. Use 'em!"

So the next time I had to report to a hospital, I did. I broke up evening traffic on the Henry Hudson Parkway and was the first person from my office to arrive. But when I told the police commissioner about my newfound skill, he replied flatly, "Don't do that." He wanted me to be safe. And I remembered police were often criticized for abusing department placards and vehicles.

Another time, after a late-night fight with my then-boyfriend, I punched the steering wheel, setting off the alarm in airhorn mode. It wouldn't stop unless the engine was running, but turning the wheel any amount—which I had to do dozens of times to get home—triggered the sirens. The fiasco sounded like a donkey was being dragged and tortured in Park Slope, Brooklyn.

My attempts to silence it proved futile, so my office called a precinct near me to help. In the time it took to lift my head from rummaging for the user manual, three patrol cars—and a cop in a golf cart!—showed up. They thought they were responding to an officer in distress and got a damsel in the headlights. Something got lost in transmission . . . but they found the fuse key and didn't make me feel like a total ass.

After other malfunctions, I was finally assigned a new edition, with upgraded lights and sirens I could select with the push of a button. The fleet director grinned when he gave me the keys. "The only thing that's the same is the color," he said. "I believe it's called champagne."

Minnette Coleman

Minnette Coleman, a member of the Harlem Writers Guild, grew up in Atlanta, Georgia, where, as a teenager, she wrote entertainment reviews for the *Atlanta Daily World.* While majoring in drama at Guilford College in Greensboro, North Carolina, she appeared in several productions and was a frequent contributor to the college newspaper. The author of three historical novels, *The Blacksmith's Daughter, No Death by Unknown Hands,* and *The Tree: A Journey to Freedom*, Minnette has been published on several websites and in the *Quaker Higher Education* journal and the *Killens Review of Arts and Letters.*

Ten Tiny Pages

Minnette Coleman

Early one steamy Southern morning in the 1960s, my father returned from the Reidsville state prison and the execution of a Black man convicted of raping a white woman. Mama had begged him not to go, fearing for his life and that of the "colored" cops with him. Wanting to be a journalist like him had kept me awake, and my dad and his police retinue shut down a local bar before he got home around 3 a.m., his shirt and tie damp, slurring his words.

I had never seen my dad drunk, and he was rambling about what happened. This cub reporter needed to hear everything about the execution, so, ignoring Mama's orders of "back to bed" while she and my burly cop godfather dealt with him, I made Dad a cup of instant coffee, black, arriving in the parlor as Uncle Howard said, "They let us in, but they wouldn't let us see the execution."

My father was furious. "They executed an innocent Black man on the tainted testimony of a white-trash hooker, and they didn't want me to cover it, didn't want it known outside the state of Georgia." He sipped the coffee, adding, "But it will be."

Originally, the woman claimed her attacker was a tall, light-skinned "Negro." The gospel singer arrested and executed was short and dark. Southern justice didn't care which Black man paid for the crime. But times were changing. From the moment of the arrest, there were rallies, fundraisers; even some local whites were petitioning for the singer's freedom. My father tirelessly attended all these gatherings and reported on how Atlanta was affecting the civil rights movement.

Animated in his drunken tirade, my father spilled his coffee on his shirt. He stood, apologizing as Mama helped him take it off. When he pulled his shirt tails from his pants, a piece of paper fell out—paper from his small notepad. He sobered up when she handed it to him.

"They were warned by the government to leave us be," he said. "That never stopped them before, so I was careful. I thought they'd take my notepad, so each time I filled a page, I'd rip it out and hide it on my person. I hid my story on me from them. I have to tell it."

Mama found a page in a rear pants pocket. Uncle Howard pulled a couple of pages from the lining of Dad's jacket, where he had loosened a thread just enough to slip them in. He hid pages in each of his socks, and I also found some inside his hat, wet with sweat but still legible.

From a pad the size of his palm, my father had produced ten tiny pages of notes. Completely clearheaded, he organized them on the coffee table, pointing out where he was in Reidsville when he made them. Exhausted from sadness, he lifted one and faced me. "When the lights flickered, we knew his end had come."

My godfather left. I made more coffee and my teary-eyed mama brought in Dad's battered Smith Corona typewriter. He wrote into the dawn, using those ten tiny pages to weave an award-winning account of racism in a time of change.

Years of awards later, *The New York Times* offered him a job as a reporter. My father, "the race man," had become city editor of the *Atlanta Daily World*, and he decided his mighty pen best served the movement in the South.

I never saw Daddy drunk again. Sometimes he'd allow me to shadow him as he covered stories. Mama approved, and she even got me a little pad like his. That night, long ago, as he documented another part of American history, he became my hero. As the sounds of his typing lulled me to sleep, I knew I'd never be able to capture a story with ten tiny pages as he did. But I think he'd be proud that he taught me enough to keep my thoughts to 650 words to tell a whole story.

Laura Shaine Cunningham

Novelist, memoirist, journalist, and playwright **Laura Shaine Cunningham** has written nine novels as well as memoirs and short plays that are often anthologized and performed around the country. In fact, her first play, *Bang*, was originally produced by Chicago's famed Steppenwolf Theatre. Her memoir *Sleeping Arrangements* was a *New York Times* bestseller, and her work appears in such notable magazines as *The New Yorker, The Atlantic,* and *Esquire*, as well as in a number of literary journals. Her latest memoir is *Forbidden Russia—An American Playwright* in *Moscow, Ukraine, Belarus and Beyond.*

Loretta Lynn: An Uncensored Memory

Laura Shaine Cunningham

"You'll never know you're not in your own bed," Loretta Lynn told me in April 1974.

We were lying on her bed, which filled the rump of her luxury tour bus—it was a king size that snapped together from the walls. The walls themselves were upholstered in puckered white leatherette and oozed recorded sound from tiny metal speaker mouths.

"Satin sheets to lie on . . ." was playing as I boarded. A row of Styrofoam heads sported her many wigs on a vanity dresser. Loretta herself was the centerpiece, wearing a sheer nightgown that revealed her Caesarean scars. Her face was ghostly and gaunt, her high cheekbones reflecting her Native American ancestry, and her voice, of course, that deep Kentucky twang. "You'll sleep in 'ere with me!" she invited. "You 'n me, we're just like sisters."

Now, Loretta Lynn has died, and I lie sleepless, remembering my nights on the road with her, when she was thirty-nine years old, and I was twenty-seven. I was on assignment for a magazine and the publicist had declared: "Loretta Lynn is a populist example of a pristine way of life."

I imagined Loretta in gingham, strumming a guitar, in a country tour bus decked out with blue checkered curtains . . . The reality was startlingly different, and I have to say—far from "pristine." I boarded the bus outside Albany and was ushered in by her bodyguard/driver, who was a big man, with an Elvis-style pompadour and a gun tucked into his armpit. He was too tall for the bus, and his hairdo flattened against the ceiling. He scratched his armpit holster and said: "Nobody write nothing bad about Loretta."

The midsection of the bus was a dorm for the band—the men lay on shelf-like beds, their cowboy boots poking out, tiny TVs dangling before their faces. Given the choice of my own shelf in this male musician dorm or accepting Loretta's invitation, I went into her bedroom.

If I ever knew I was not in my own bed, it was on those nights I traveled with Loretta—going over 100 miles per hour, her meals of chili, coconut cream custard pie, and soda spilled across the mattress on the faster turns. Along with nonstop confessions: Loretta was instantly unexpurgated. Her marriage, she said, was worse than depicted. "Crazy ole mens," she summed it up, "all they know is they got a long thing 'n wimmins got a hole to put it in . . ."

"He's cheating all the time. For years, I had a girl detective follow him, and then she slept with him too. I had a stack of photos, and then I thought—*What am I collecting them for?*" To say that she and her late husband did not get along is an understatement. "I was in a boat with him when it turned over, and he dove into the water to save the cooler, not me."

Then she handed me the most recent magazine article about her and asked, "Does it say anything about orgasms?"

I was stunned that she was so open and unguarded. It's what a journalist hopes for and seldom gets, but she was so warm and welcoming despite her obvious confusion, I said, "You know, you can be more careful. If you don't want to see something in print, you can say: 'Off the record.'"

She nodded, but I wasn't sure she retained the information. But later, when we stopped to pick up a male country star and he jumped into bed too, they flew into an immediate embrace . . . I bunched up against the far wall. She looked over his shoulder, winked at me, and said, "Off the record."

I got off her bus at a stop in Flint, Michigan. She called after me to "Stay!"

What stayed is the memory of her kindness and confusion, her being either unable or unwilling to dissemble. She was a rare woman, indeed, and today, I do mourn her.

Kathy Curto

Kathy Curto teaches at the Writing Institute at Sarah Lawrence College and Montclair State University as well as several nonprofit organizations and writing centers in the metropolitan area. She is the author of *Not for Nothing: Glimpses into a Jersey Girlhood*. Kathy's column—Words on the Street, Revisited—is featured biweekly in *Write or Die Magazine.* Her piece "Still Cooking Side by Side," considered a "Modern Love in miniature" by *The New York Times*, was included in *The Best of Tiny Love Stories* in August 2021. Kathy lives in the Hudson Valley with her family and can be found in her front yard on most mornings, replenishing her Little Free Library with donated books. This practice has become one of her daily delights.

What He Knew

Kathy Curto

The kids were one, three, five, and six. We had no business going away with them in tow, but we were trying to stay sane and in love, so we went anyway. I wanted no laundry and a meal I didn't cook. He wanted a break from work. And the kids wanted to take turns pushing a hotel elevator button. I booked a place, Mountaintop Lodge, ninety minutes away with a room that fit us all. I didn't ask about dress codes. I didn't ask about dinner seating. I didn't ask about what I now know are defined as *additional charges*.

In the lobby we were greeted with an onslaught of pastel sweater sets and loafers. Lots and lots of loafers. My faded jean jacket was clearly the wrong call. All eyes were on the jacket and my son, Sam. His Buzz Lightyear pajamas smelled sour, and Buzz's face was stained with a blob of Yoo-hoo. Hushed remarks about the girls, too, were likely—with their uneven ponytails and stick-on fake fingernail tips in neon colors.

I thought this was a *lodge*. To me, lodge meant jeans, hot dogs, and s'mores. Not pressed khakis, beef Wellington, and petit fours. Or afternoon tea.

"One or two keys, sir?" Audrey, the reservation specialist, asked my husband, Peppe.

"Two's good," he answered and signed the card that allowed us to charge our every move. Because, in addition to looking nothing like a lodge, Mountaintop also didn't match my idea of what a lodge costs. There would be no cherries in the Shirley Temples for us.

We got through dinner probably because we employed Operation If You Behave as a means of survival. The kids wanted to play after, so we rolled out our favorite strategy: leverage.

Earlier, Audrey had told us all about the "magnificent" game room. "And for your little princesses we have *spectacular* costumes!" Audrey winked, too, but looked away when she noticed two of our three princesses picking their noses.

So after dinner we went to the game room, where they played dress-up and Cinderella pinball. There was even a make-your-own cotton candy machine, which is just what their already inappropriate outfits didn't need.

We were *done*.

But as we left, we noticed a dim backroom. Inside, a pool table.

"When was the last time you played pool?" Peppe asked.

"College, I think," I said, realizing what that meant. We had never played pool together.

"How about one game?" he nudged.

The kids were tired and sticky. But some higher power pulled them onto the fancy leather couch next to the pool table. They curled up into one another and squealed.

"No, let me watch you," I said and sat on a stool in the corner next to the sticks and chalk and ball racks. I had forgotten something about myself, but when he reached for the cue stick I was reminded.

There's a slow, smooth, deliberate manner of leaning that must happen to play pool well. He knew about that.

Then there are the ways hands and fingers and legs must work to play the game. Knew that, too.

There are the sounds. The cracks and echoes that arouse, thrill, and startle. The breaks, stunts, and tricks. There's the jukebox and there's Muddy Waters.

There are the eyes. How they watch, deepen, and consider. And the way they shift up, just before the shot, maybe to see who's watching.

He looked up at me and let his cue slide forward. My eyes dwelled on his for a handful of seconds and then an epiphany: I may not have gotten off the stool, but we were both playing in this game.

Still.

I gazed from him to the kids, who were tangled up and almost asleep on Mountaintop's fancy leather couch.

I watched him some more.

And there, in my faded jean jacket, I was shaken and stirred.

Karen Dukess

Karen Dukess is the author of *The Last Book Party*, which was an Indie Next and Discover New Writers pick. Her new novel, *Welcome to Murder Week*, was published in summer 2025 by Scout Press, an imprint of Simon & Schuster. Karen is also the host of The Castle Hill Author Talks, a series of virtual and in-person interviews with some of today's most exciting authors. Karen has been a tour guide in the former Soviet Union, a newspaper reporter in Florida, a magazine publisher in Russia, and, for nearly a decade, a speechwriter on gender equality for the United Nations Development Programme. She has blogged on raising boys for *The Huffington Post* and written book reviews for *USA Today*. She has a degree in Russian studies from Brown University and a master's in journalism from Columbia University. She lives with her family near New York City and spends as much time as possible in Truro on Cape Cod.

The Girl in the Back Office

Karen Dukess

On summer mornings at Motif Designs, women in tennis skirts flipped through fat books of Marimekko wallpaper. With tilted heads and pursed lips, they contemplated the implications of choosing the cheerful orange poppies instead of the sophisticated green ferns. They scrutinized nearly identical paint chips and asked if venetian blinds would make the right statement for the living room.

I was seventeen and had interest in none of it. Working in the back office, I was bored—in a 1980, pre-iPhone, pre–texting friends from the bathroom, pre–Candy Crush kind of way. Just me and a pile of invoices and purchase orders, an adding machine that chewed up rolls of paper, and a slow, noisy fax machine. The job's saving grace was that it was mindless enough for daydreaming. As I typed up estimates, my mind drifted to memories of the nights before, when I'd snuck into Manor Park with my boyfriend, and thoughts of the days to come, when I would finally leave home for college. I didn't know precisely what I wanted from the future, but I knew it would involve writing, adventure, and romance; would take place nowhere near suburban Larchmont, New York; and would never require the services of an interior decorator.

One morning, I peeked out from the back office to see the store owner consulting with a man with jet-black hair and dark sunglasses.

It was our local celebrity, Eyewitness News anchor Ernie Anastos. With shades remaining on, Anastos joined his wife in discussing new decor for their home, a stone house with turrets that stood at the end of a winding driveway behind a tall iron gate. I knew the house well; as a girl, whenever we'd drive by, I'd strain my neck to look at the castle, hoping to see the princess who lived there.

Now, I was less impressed. Watching the couple finger fabric swatches, I whispered to the twenty-something office manager, "If I ever end up anything like them, someone had better just shoot me."

You know where this is going, right?

As I type, I'm in my house, about six miles from the site of Motif Designs, where there is now a bank. My husband is at work, reporting on the economy for cable television. One son is down the road in high school, the other across the country in college. I am back at my laptop after taking a short break to have flat Roman shades, selected with the help of a decorator, installed in my bedroom.

Is the ambitious girl in the back room at Motif Designs disappointed? Probably.

I'm pretty sure she would be pleased to know she would get romance and adventure: A newspaper job in a swampy Florida town, years working in Russia, and marriage to the adventurous guy who was willing to go along for the ride. But she would be aghast to learn that by her mid-thirties, she would move to the suburbs, where she would raise two children and work a mommy-track job everyone would say she was lucky to have.

For much of my adult life, I had that girl on my shoulder—sometimes pushing me forward, occasionally holding me back with her naive beliefs that learning the art of compromise is not a good thing, that a twenty-five-year marriage can't possibly be romantic, and that you can't have flat Roman shades and be a writer.

But as I neared fifty, I had an epiphany: I'm wiser than a seventeen-year-old girl, and old enough to tell her to shut up. And when I did just that, the best of her spirit came through. So now, when I sit down to work on the novel I am finally writing and determined to finish, I can hear her girlish voice, brash and hopeful, urging me on.

Lynn Edelson

Lynn Edelson has been writing memoir for more than fifteen years. Her narrative essays have appeared in the NYC Listen To Your Mother show, *Writers Read's* Carnegie Hall Voices of Hope festival, HerStry blog, Every Family's Got One, and *The Westchester Review.* She was also a finalist for the 2023 Eunice Williams Nonfiction Prize. Lynn is the mother of two grown sons, who now have their own kids. She lives in the Hudson Valley with her husband and their very bad dog.

Counterpoint

Lynn Edelson

"Here?" Arthur asks, pointing to an open space.

"Looks good," I say.

Our husbands nod in agreement as they drop the bags of food and sand chairs to the grass. We set up our things, and even though the sun is in our eyes, we're happy to be finally sitting down. I place myself between Arthur and my husband and reach for the bag of chips.

Yo-Yo Ma is closing out the season at Tanglewood with the Bach Project, and the lawns are packed with $15-ticket holders.

As the sun begins to set, the landscape darkens. Loud applause echoes as Yo-Yo Ma walks out onto the empty stage, bows, and smiles at us all. He sits down on the lone chair that stands behind the cello. A hush falls over the crowd as his bow moves across the strings.

I am entranced. Bach is my go-to guy, the one who fills me up when the days are longer and the nights are darker, when the quiet echoes within. The mathematics are seductive; the counterpoint melodies keep me spellbound. I reach for my husband's hand, because only he knows how joyful I am feeling.

It is not until the end of the fourth suite that Yo-Yo Ma finally speaks. He thanks us for being there, for supporting this international project to heal political divisiveness, for bearing witness. Then he introduces the next suite.

"This one is especially meaningful for me," he tells us. "When I'm feeling depressed, or in need of renewal, this is the piece I go to for solace. So, this is dedicated to all of those who have experienced loss. The loss of health, of love, the loss of dignity."

I am stunned by his words.

He is speaking directly to my heart. The heart that is trying to wrap itself around my son, who is struggling to find his way as he moves past the life he shared with the woman he loved. I am sitting in the dark thinking about my child, the one who hears all the words not spoken, the one who cannot yet envision a future without her by his side.

I am no longer holding my husband's hand. I am trying to breathe into the night, holding on to the stars, holding on to a whisper of hope.

Yo-Yo Ma moves through the piece with tenderness and begins the final suite, but I can't keep up. I am still caught up in his words, in the gentle nod of his head, until the music finally stops and he speaks to us again.

"Thank you, thank you," he begins.

And then he talks about Tanglewood, about the impact it has had on the culture, and especially about the opportunities it provides young musical talent.

"And to that end," he says with a grin, "we found someone who wrote a wonderful song at the age of twenty. May I introduce to you, Jimmy Taylor."

And out walks James Taylor onto the stage. The crowd gasps, erupts in applause, and starts calling his name. He sits on a stool very close to Yo-Yo Ma and they begin to play "Sweet Baby James." The audience begins cheering as James Taylor is singing, until they finally settle into the music.

And me? I am weeping. My hands are in my lap, my fists are tight, and I am smiling as tears are streaming down my cheeks and all I can think about is magic.

This moment, the joy of this surprise.

I am sobbing silently into the darkness, even as everyone around me is laughing and singing along. And I am filled up with love and the hope that perhaps, just perhaps, those magical moments are still out there for my son. That they will come upon him when he's not looking, when he has given up, when he can no longer see the stars.

Honor Finnegan

Honor Finnegan is a preschool special educator, Heartfulness meditation trainer, and mother to one adult son. She currently resides in Ithaca, New York, after relocating from New York City via a string of interim abodes including Dubai and India. Past incarnations include child performer (first national tour of *Annie*); improv pioneer (*Honor Versus the Brain of the Galaxy* by Del Close); jail bird (Holloway Women's Prison, Greenham Common Peace Camp); Galway blow-in busker, band member, and musical society secret weapon (Galway, Ireland); quirky singer-songwriter (Kerrville New Folk winner); and *Moth* storyteller (NYC and a couple of almost-mainstages—one of these days!). Honor loves *Writers Read.*

Money

Honor Finnegan

I married into Money. Literally. That was the family name. They were English, from Southampton, the city that launched the Titanic. I glanced at a stack of his mail, and at first I thought it was a joke: Mr. Money.

Mr. Money was a penny-pinching fiscal neurotic who had a lot of anxiety about . . . money. He was always very concerned that everything be 50/50, and so for nearly twenty years of marriage we had separate bank accounts.

I met Mr. Money in Ireland, at Monroe's Tavern in Galway City, across the street from the Arch View hostel where I worked. He played guitar in a blues band. I asked if I could get up and sing. The front man said yes; Mr. Money said no. The front man won.

I was small, quiet, and unassuming, until I hit the stage. I stood in the front of that packed pub, tapped out the tempo to the band, and sang "Wild Women Don't Have the Blues," by Ida Cox: "I've got a disposition and a way of my own. When my man starts kicking, I let him find another home . . ."

I tore it up. Brought down the house. Standing ovation. They never saw it coming, including Mr. Money. I walked off stage and straight out the door. It was a dramatic exit, but I was tired and wanted to get to bed. The next morning Mr. Money came looking for me. He wanted to start a new blues band. I wanted to sing Irish music, but I went with it: A gig's a gig, and it beat working at the hostel. The Irish love the blues, and a pub owner picked the name: The Honorary Blues Band.

Mr. Money was very pretty—a delicate Mick Jagger in a gray leather jacket. We brought out the worst in each other and fought from day one. One night we had a situation that required the morning-after medication. He said he would pay for half. It had to be 50/50. The drug was nauseating, his stance infuriating. I flew into a rage and set the tone of our relationship.

We got pregnant later. It was a mutual, intentional accident. He wanted to be a father. I wanted to be a mother. We wanted to play music. We thought we'd make a go of it, so Mr. Money and I were married in the last trimester, splitting the cost of the license 50/50. The Money in-laws came over. They referred to England as the mainland. They made my Irish roots shudder. I made their stiff upper lips quiver. I kept my name, Finnegan, and we all kept our distance.

Mr. Money and I moved to New York City and raised our baby. Our first neighborhood was Bay Ridge in Brooklyn, where I waited tables at a diner. While Mr. Money lived off his separate savings, I saved receipts for household items, to prove I was pulling my weight, 50/50. We won a housing lottery and moved to Chelsea. Our baby went to elementary school, middle school, and high school. Then our baby went to college, and the apartment was empty—just me and Mr. Money, living 50/50. It turns out that two halves do not make a whole.

The divorce was uncontested. It cost $500. That was $250, each.

Joanna FitzPatrick

Joanna FitzPatrick was born and raised in Hollywood. So it is perhaps no surprise that her first writing forays were screenplays. But Joanna also flourished in the music business, a job that brought her frequently to New York City, where she could embrace the city's nightlife: dancing till dawn, all-night jam sessions, hailing midnight taxis. All of this was a welcome escape from what was, to her, California's excessive sunshine. Along the way she raised two children and finished her education, including an MFA in creative writing from Sarah Lawrence College. Joanna has written several novels, including her most recent, *The Artist Colony*, a historical mystery set in Carmel-by-the-Sea.

Basking in Divine Light

Joanna FitzPatrick

In the sixties and seventies in Hollywood, we women in music were women in bed with musicians, or we were groupies, or we danced in cages at Whisky a Go Go, or, like me, we were humble servants for showbiz bosses who ran the show.

I had just been hired by one of those bosses. I didn't have any experience as a secretary, but my mother had made sure I was a fast typist and a shorthand star. "Something to fall back on," she'd said, as if she knew I'd be divorced and destitute before I turned thirty.

My first assignment was to pick up my boss's client arriving from New York at the Los Angeles airport. "How will I recognize her?" I asked.

He said, "You can't miss her."

In the crowded arrival hallway, I dropped my sign when a spiritual vision in neon came into my sight. A tiny person with breasts bubbling like uncorked champagne from the tight bodice of her flaring red dress strutted toward me in glittery red platform shoes and flaming red hair. She was everything I wasn't: exuberant, extravagant, joyous, and wildly independent. Need I ask her if she was the Divine Miss M?

At rehearsals, I watched her do her own choreography. She knew what she wanted, and she got it from her manager and everyone else who worked with her, not by coercion or intimidation but through her unique brand of integrity. She treated her backup singers, the Harlettes, and the musicians and the stagehands with dignity. We were all part of the show, and we loved it. And we loved her.

Several months later I achieved the impossible, or so thought my boss. I not only organized his messy office, but as Bette's watchdog, I sheltered her through an emergency appendectomy by keeping her fans away from the hospital, and I gave Bette her first driving lesson.

The boss gave me a bonus and then ordered a limo to bring me to Bette's concert on New Year's Eve, 1975. Serendipity! A previously unemployed single mom raising a six-year-old daughter without alimony or child support was stepping into a limo and sinking into its plush leather seat.

My skin-tight bronze satin jumpsuit and three-inch gold lamé stilettos sparkled as I flew through the night in my black-winged chariot sipping champagne, blasting Bette singing "Friends" on the stereo, and thinking life couldn't get any better than this.

My seat was second-row center in the sold-out, three-thousand-seat Dorothy Chandler Pavilion. The curtain went up, and Bette, seductively stretched out on a hospital bed, was rolled out on stage. (Her original concert dates had been postponed after her appendectomy.) In a flash, she was off that bed and strutting across the massive stage in her chunky platform shoes, pouring her heart into every lyric of "Do You Want to Dance?"

Throughout her two-and-a-half-hour performance, Bette released her exuberant, compassionate spirit into the rafters, and I sucked it in until it became my own. She filled me with her impassioned voice until I heard my own. And like her, I knew I could survive the slings and arrows thrown by those who were afraid of my strength, of her strength. We had a job to do, and we could do it together.

After going backstage and telling her how much I loved her show, I strode out of that theater in my silky jumpsuit, aware of the stares I received as I slipped into the waiting limo. Everyone thought I was somebody, but more importantly, I thought so too!

That night I realized I didn't need a man to live an exciting, creative life. I didn't need his limelight to bring me out of the dark. I had my own light. I just had to open the door and let it out. And the Divine Miss M had shown me exactly how to do that.

Christine Koubek Flynn

Christine Koubek Flynn is a mother of sons, a writer, a teacher, and a caffeinated runner who loves working with people in writing workshops, including through the Armed Services Arts Partnership. She was adopted and raised in New York. But she was born in Massachusetts, where she lived while in her twenties, and this turned her into—she's almost afraid to admit this here—a Red Sox fan. She holds an MFA in creative writing from Fairfield University. Her work has appeared in *The Washington Post* and *Poets & Writers*. She has received awards from the American Society of Journalists and Authors as well as the Elizabeth George Foundation for her novel-in-progress.

A Baby from the Back Row

Christine Koubek Flynn

We spend nearly forty weeks of our lives underwater, in a cocoon of warmth and darkness. The experts say we develop faster in the womb than at any other time in our lives, and that we spend those last weeks absorbing noises and smells, sensing our mother's moods, and gathering intel on our soon-to-be environment. If this is true, then I sensed from within that first clandestine space that something was amiss.

I might have had an inkling that my mother was an uptown girl, her plaid-pleated skirt swishing side to side as she hurried through the hallways of her late-1960s Catholic girls' school in upstate New York. My heartbeat likely raced with hers the day a classmate caught her vomiting in the bathroom.

The school nurse called her mother. The voices that night were furious.

And again two days later when her parents found us sitting on a park bench with the boy who got her pregnant. She and I were four months together then—and on a bus the next day, destined for her older sister's house in Maryland, she with a phony wedding ring and her father's parting instructions: "Tell anyone who asks that your husband is in Vietnam."

Upheaval followed each trimester: first the move to Maryland, then to Massachusetts, a colder, sequestered place in the Berkshire mountains, where there were suddenly more voices like hers.

As the weeks wore on and I grew larger, we were two parts of one whole. I was a place she rested her forearms as she learned to knit soft scarves, a muse for poems I would one day read, and a captive audience as her fingers raced across piano keys practicing Chopin, Rachmaninoff, and Beethoven's "Moonlight Sonata." Sometimes she hummed along.

Her music and alto voice were my growing limbic system's soundtrack, the part of me primed to hear which person in a room of strangers was her. She had a stomachache after indulging in chocolate on Halloween night.

She thought it was indigestion. I was born the next day.

I imagine I was lulled by all that felt familiar in the short time my mother held me close. She touched each of my fingers and toes. And then the connection with her, the music, stopped.

What happened next, I discovered two decades later, happened to more than two million babies born in America in the years before *Roe v. Wade*. I was swaddled in a blanket, in one of the hospital nursery's back-row bassinets, alongside the other illegitimates.

She returned home from the hospital and told her friends that she was finally over a horrific case of mono. I spent my first trimester out of the womb at a Catholic orphanage.

By January's end, a Sister dressed in black and white handed my adoptive parents an amended birth certificate and placed me in my new mother's arms, saying, "Here, it's as if you gave birth to her yourself."

They thought we were blank slates.

I still wonder sometimes who took care of all those babies, who fed us and loved us before we were adopted. There are no stories, no notes on first smiles. I realized this one cloudless night as I breastfed my newborn son near my bedroom window.

His little fist reached up and clung to a curl of my hair, as if to say, "I belong. I belong to you." I studied his round, pink face illuminated by the moonlight. I touched each of his sausage-shaped toes. I couldn't imagine untangling my hair from his fingers to hand him over, never to smell his powdery soft skin again or know the person he would become. And I wondered what it was like for my first mother—for Ann.

How do you surrender your baby? How do you live forward in a fiction?

And what does it do to a person—to us—in the end?

Sharon Forman

Sharon Forman is a reform rabbi, teacher, writer, and mother. Raised in Norfolk, Virginia, she holds degrees from Yale University, Columbia Teachers College, and Hebrew Union College-Jewish Institute of Religion. Her writing can be found on- and offline, including a Tiny Love Story in *The New York Times,* in *Literary Mama*, and on jewishfiction.net. Her short play, *Elisheva*, was performed in 2022 at the Jewish Theatre of Oklahoma. Sharon has also published *The Baseball Haggadah: A Festival of Freedom and Springtime in 15 Innings*. She lives with her husband and baseball-obsessed children in Westchester, New York, where she teaches bar and bat mitzvah students.

Ghosts at the Costco

Sharon Forman

Ten thirty at night, and the house is quiet. At his desk, my husband, a cardiologist, studies a stack of electrocardiograms, his pen circling suspicious troughs and peaks, the steady or interrupted drumming of another heartbeat.

I fight off sudden chills. I'm a practical woman and a rabbi who does not waste energy worrying about what comes after this life. Yet now, in the silence of my home, I wonder if I, too, have begun to detect the echoes of distant heartbeats. I wonder if I believe in ghosts.

Until that day nearly a decade ago, I'd never been able to explain the dread that overtakes me whenever I approach our local Costco, an innocuous giant box store with gray cement walls and abundant towers of triple-fudge brownie mix. But before I even get out of my car, a magnetic tug propels me to flee.

That winter morning, I was determined to conquer any disturbing sensations and restock our pantry with enough frozen waffles to open my own pancake house. But as soon as I entered the cavernous warehouse, it began again: My hands tingled with electric shocks when I grasped the shopping cart. An inexplicable sadness settled over me. My chest throbbed, as if I needed to nurse a hungry infant. Was I experiencing an anxiety attack? Was I losing my mind?

By the time I returned home, my heart ached so much I could hardly breathe. I swallowed two of the 1,200 ibuprofen tablets I had just purchased and turned to my computer. Maybe Facebook would distract my racing thoughts.

Coincidentally, a friend had just posted about another Costco, praising the store's expansive kosher selections. I commented sourly: "Does anyone else feel ill at the Costco in Westchester?"

Later that night, I returned to Facebook and read a stranger's startling response: "I never go to that Westchester Costco because of all that business with the Jewish cemetery."

About four seconds of detective work on the computer unspooled the mystery. For one hundred years, a synagogue and its cemetery overlooked the Yonkers hill where the Costco now stands. Unable to afford the cemetery upkeep, the few elderly surviving members gave their land to developers—but only in exchange for a promise: that the cemetery's inhabitants, including 147 children, would be reburied in Jerusalem. A recent investigation revealed that the remains of only 12 could be accounted for in Israel. The balance on that receipt included 135 dead Jewish children's remains lying beneath the concrete floor where I had just pushed my shopping cart.

I close my laptop and sit down on the couch to fold the laundry, still warm from the dryer. My hands fold and crease, flattening my son's pants, reuniting my daughter's pink socks. If only my mind could be smoothed so easily. But I cannot stop thinking about those children.

Perhaps I sensed their presence because I'm so attuned to the past, to the ways it persists into the present. As a Jew, I am commanded to remember. Sabbaths, festivals, tyrants, covenants, commandments—all are supposed to be engraved in memory, a heavy habit passed through generations, as enduring as the physical attributes we inherit: a widow's peak, long toes, an allergy to the bumpy skin of strawberries. Who or what remembered me as I stood on that old, sacred ground?

After millions of years on this planet, I suppose we are all walking over the bones of each other. Yet, it's only the souls of these motherless children who call to me, whose presence on that windy hill triggers my restless heartbeat.

I wish I knew how to honor them, these long-dead children, whose mothers surely loved them as fiercely as I love mine. But I can only murmur the words my people have always uttered in the face of loss, the blessing recited upon hearing of a death: Baruch Dayan Ha-Emet.

Blessed is the True Judge.

Debra Fried

Debra Fried lives in Greenwich Village with her husband and just-post-college twins, and is very happy when she's reading, baking, or riding a bike on a boardwalk. She's spent the past twenty-five years working in advertising as a creative director. The work she's most known for (and most proud of) is the launch of Dove's award-winning Campaign for Real Beauty. In addition to widening the parameters of beauty, she's done her part to widen America's hips and put baubles onto its wrists, with advertising for clients that run the gamut from Hellmann's Mayonnaise to Tiffany & Co. Debra has a newsletter on Substack, where she writes about "clothing and life, but not in that order," and has been published by *The New York Times*.

Filippo's, Can I Help You?

Debra Fried

The phones ring madly because it's Friday night. I punch the first blinking light and grab a pizza box, anchoring the receiver between my chin and shoulder.

"Filippo's, can I help you?" I ask. I scribble "Large Mushroom" on the box and say "half an hour" into the phone. We always say half an hour, no matter what. I scrawl the address, then punch the other blinking buttons.

As I do the phones, Angelo, the youngest and most handsome of the crew, shouts orders to Filippo and Vincenzo, who slap disks of dough onto the counter, spreading them outward with their fingertips. They lift the dough high, stretching it between their hands, like strings in a game of Cat's Cradle. Angelo removes pies from the oven and cuts them into eighths, making a crispy sound that I love.

I'm the American college girl who cramps their style—with me, they can't talk about the new strip club that just opened on Route 35 and they're forced to speak English. Which reduces us to stilted conversations about mozzarella deliveries.

It's odd to work with people you don't know, but I gather things. Filippo is shy, but tough. Vincenzo, the oldest, is the funniest. When he tells stories, they lean in, smile expectantly as he pauses before a punchline, then throw their heads back and roar. Angelo has the shortest fuse. When a customer takes too long, or has an attitude, his jaw tenses and he taps his fingers on the counter, muttering in a way that makes the others step in. Angelo doesn't speak much English, but he loves the word *asshole*.

Night shifts fly.

Sunday afternoons are different. We amble in and take our places at the counter. We slowly open cans of peppers and stick tabs into slots, turning sheets of cardboard into the boxes that I'll scribble orders onto later. The air is scented with rosemary and garlic, onions, and lemons—lighter and fresher than the essence of mozzarella and tomato that constantly clings to me. On Sundays, the men cook. Not for customers; for us.

Here, I first taste focaccia, warm and crispy, with a drizzle of olive oil, baked by Vincenzo. And Angelo's chicken, roasted with lemons and onions. The place feels different when they cook. Slower. Sweeter. Quieter.

Filippo loves "Lay Down Sally" by Eric Clapton, but apparently thinks Sally is an elderly Jewish man who needs a nap. "Play 'Lay Down Saul,'" he says, handing me quarters from the register. I return from the jukebox as Filippo, humming along, cuts a red onion into thin slices, scattering them onto a salad like a dealer with a deck of cards.

Angelo pushes tables together. Vincenzo opens a bottle of red, and Filippo steps from the oven, holding a baking dish between oven-mitted hands. He smiles shyly as he sets the lasagna down. It is meltingly good, and we eat in silence. Finally, I say, "Filippo, this is amazing."

He ducks his head.

"My mother's recipe," he says softly. His eyes shine, and the others nod with quiet appreciation.

"My mother uses lots of ricotta too," Angelo says. Vincenzo talks about his mother's olive oil cake, giving his curled-in fingers a kiss.

"My mother uses a little coffee when she braises beef," Filippo says, in an almost-whisper. I say mine does that with brisket. Our eyes meet. And we're at ease.

At this table, they're not hot-tempered men who yell at idiots and go to strip clubs. They're boys. Boys who love their mothers. Boys who miss home. We sing along to "Lay Down Saul" and sip our wine until the phone rings.

"Filippo's, can I help you?" I say.

I scribble the order, then return to the table.

Pizza can wait.

It's Sunday.

And we're eating.

Wendy Goldman

Born in Chicago, the daughter of a funny mother, **Wendy Goldman** would hop the el downtown to study improv at Second City. She was hooked. Wendy began her career as an actress and company member of famed LA comedy troupe The Groundlings. She and fellow Groundling Judy Toll created an original musical—so they could have really big parts and sing in front of a large group of people. A surprise hit, the award-winning *Casual Sex* launched their film adaptation for producer Ivan Reitman and Universal Studios. Wendy went on to have a long career as a writer-producer on loads of TV shows, but she continues to improvise her way through life. In addition to her ongoing writing pursuits, Wendy currently teaches workshops here in New York and inspires creativity as a writing coach. But despite her years living in other cities, she refuses to lose her Chicago accent.

The Actual Brentwood

Wendy Goldman

It's been over a month since I told my therapist I was leaving, but I can't yet, because she needs me too much. The problem is her fifteen-year-old daughter. Who used to get good grades, and they used to be so close. Now they're barely speaking. I can tell from Marcia's cold that won't go away, this daughter stuff is really killing her. I slide the Kleenex box across the coffee table in her direction.

Before the session, I saw that same woman in the lobby in the purple sweatsuit. For years now, same bench. Cuddling a stuffed elephant. Makes me think: "Well, as crappy as I'm doing, at least . . ." This time, though, the elephant was inside her knapsack with only its trunk hanging out. Progress. Plus, she was chatting with somebody on her cell. I think there was somebody on the other end.

Progress is why I decided to leave Marcia. I pictured her happy about it, or at least okay. Dream analysis isn't her "strength," she said so herself, and my dreams mean a lot. Instead, she insists we need more sessions to wrap things up. For my sake. My stomach, which she taught me to listen to, is screaming "No!" and one time I forgot to sign the check. But every Tuesday, I'm back in the elevator, pressing three.

Her daughter will be better off in boarding school. Although it's not going to be easy on anyone. "I can imagine," is what I say and nod along. When she sighs, and it's quiet, I jump in: "So, I actually think I'm ready for this to be our last session together." Marcia looks confused. Then like I'd slapped her. "This is what you do. You cut people off cold!" Me? No. Me? But her eyes are already darting toward the clock I can't see on the bookshelf. "That's our time for today. We'll pick this up again next week."

After that, I pass two business guys on San Vicente, shaking their heads. "Good thing it's not my car." "Shit, yeah." It hits me—I bet I'm getting a ticket. I start running.

A young girl shrieks, "Do you believe it?" She points to a gigantic tree branch blocking the sidewalk. It's crushing a VW Bug at the curb. You can only see the license plate. 6RBT552. I swear this is a perfectly clear California day. No wind. No storm. No earthquake. Now I really run.

My car . . .

If this were a dream, my legs would turn to cement. Or I'd be in a public restroom with an overflowing toilet. Not my fault, but I've gotta clean up the mess. Or I'm trapped in a dark alley with a man with claws for hands. But this isn't a dream. It's the actual Brentwood. Not a nightmare Brentwood. And I'm truly wide awake.

I wait an hour for AAA. Police cordon off the street. Everybody's gotta honk their horns and stare. Person after person walks by and moans: "Thank God, it's not me!" I wear big sunglasses, but not big enough to hide my entire face and body.

Luckily the cab of the tow truck smells like French fries, which is a comfort. I'm convinced the tree falling on my car is a sign from the universe. I will never, ever, park on San Vicente again. In fact, I will avoid the entire area of Marcia's office. A five-block radius. Six.

I'm already dialing her number. She sounds lonely on her voice mail, but I can't worry about that now. "I'm canceling our session next Tuesday. Thank you for all your help. But I'm not coming ever again. Anymore. Really. For sure. Bye. I mean it."

I gaze at my phone like any minute it'll turn to gold or dance around in my hand. Did I just say that?

Progress.

Sometimes all it takes is a little nudge.

Alison Gragnano

Alison Gragnano is executive creative director at The New School/ Parsons, a position she says she obtained by way of a brutal yet thrilling thirty-some-odd-year career in advertising, with over a decade split between two agencies alone, Saatchi and Saatchi and Ogilvy and Mather. Alison leads an in-house agency in the development of all marketing and communications for the university, collaborating with a team of talented and passionate creatives to share the vision and mission of The New School, a place for fearless progress and a university that includes: Parsons School of Design, the number one design school in the U.S.; Eugene Lang College of Liberal Arts; College of Performing Arts; The New School for Social Research; Schools of Public Engagement; Parsons Paris; and Continuing & Professional Education.

The Italian Heart

Alison Gragnano

23andMe confirms what my Piedmontese mother has always told me: I am 95 percent Italian. I am a disparate and always conflicted mixture of the austere northern Italian blood of my mother and my father's more accepting and warm southern blood. I am currently a creative director at The New School/Parsons. I got there by way of a brutal yet thrilling thirty-some-odd-year career in advertising. This story tells the tale of a volunteering project I signed up for to wash those years of advertising right out of my hair. I love Italy. I am going there tomorrow. But it is not the Italy of the movies. It is the Italy of a complex nation in flux, with the most beautiful heritage and past and a future that is yet to be determined. I tried to capture that Italy in this short piece. A story of tough-hearted but kind people who are trying to adjust to a world they know nothing about.

Sometimes technology will break your heart.

Google Translate worked quickly, revealing the English words for Bengali: "But no one will ever love me. I am poor and I am brown." I typed back equally fast, "You are wrong, you are beautiful and young. You will not always be poor."

I was taking a break from the soulless world of advertising, volunteering in Calabria with an Italian nongovernmental organization (NGO) that was aiding the massive refugee population entering the country. But I was not prepared for the complexities I was about to encounter.

Our group was assigned to a home for "unaccompanied minors." We volunteers were a motley crew, ranging from a spoiled American gap-year kid to an eighty-two-year-old British retiree and everything in between. I had imagined nestling small children, teaching them a song, or serving them a snack.

But when we pulled up to the farmhouse, we saw an aggressive game of soccer being played by a group of man-boys.

Yes, they were all under the age of eighteen, hence the *minor* distinction, but these were not children. They were teenagers who had traveled for weeks through deserts in Africa, mountains in Bangladesh, and treacherous seas in Libya to arrive here in Italy.

Wearing fake Gucci and Balenciaga, dressed in hipster sneakers, they just wanted to forget their terrifying journeys, seeking solace in a soccer game, speaking the international language of testosterone and survival.

On the sidelines were the fragile boys, the ones who had somehow survived but were broken, missing home, and completely at a loss, texting with me and Google Translate.

The farm was run by two locals. Louis, the teacher, had grown up in this remote little town. He treated the boys with the respect and discipline characteristic of an old-world teacher. Sophia, the cook, prepared three meals a day for these twenty-three boys and, with a glance, a gesture, or a bowl of rigatoni, shared the unspoken kindness of an austere and undemonstrative aunt.

These boys had left their families thousands of miles away. They'd traveled for weeks—in one case, five months—without exchanging a single word with the parents they might never see again. When these unaccompanied minors arrived by boat, they were greeted by UN workers in this region of Italy that had been decimated by its own long exodus dating back many years, an exodus of youth. These villages were now populated solely by old people. Our town had 250 residents remaining. With the help of the UN, they built immaculate apartments in their ancient stone village and furnished them to house 150 Syrian and African refugees. In effect, this meant giving over their village to "others," people from "away"—with different customs, religions, and codes of conduct. These Italians were extremely poor, wearing ragged, moth-eaten sweaters to church, but they also wore the kindness of people who had suffered, and they treated these "others" with stoic and genuine kindness.

Typical teenagers, the refugees were desperate to leave this rural place. They felt trapped and desperate. They wanted adventure, to travel to Paris, to Rome, to the countries they had seen in movies. They were looking forward to turning eighteen, to no longer being unaccompanied minors, to the freedom to leave this place.

When they are old enough to look back, I hope they will remember their time in this remote, rugged village with warmth. Despite their poverty and old age, these villagers let the boys slip into their craggy hearts. They developed a reluctant love for them and showed that love through food, their daily greetings, the way they protected them and shared their homes with them.

I saw it. Clearly. I hoped that someday, the boys would see it too.

John Gredler

John Gredler has, for most of his adult life, been filling notebooks and journals, most recently from his home in Tuckahoe, New York. Luckily, his private musings have often led to poems, memoir, stories, and essays that all of us can enjoy. Which is to say that he has published widely in such places as *Atticus Review, Fictionique, Narratively, Talking Writing,* and *Dan's Papers*. John studied at Bella Villa Writers, the Terzo Piano Workshops, and the Writing Institute at Sarah Lawrence College, where he was honored with the 2014 Kathryn Gurfein Fellowship. While John's love of the written word is boundless, he also understands that sometimes less is more and in 2016 won an Honorable Mention in the *Westchester Review*'s flash fiction contest.

Ashtray

John Gredler

The day after, it was like nothing had happened. I came downstairs and saw the ashtray in its usual place on the coffee table. I looked around for signs of damage but found none.

The ashtray was heavy, translucent green glass. The sunlight coming in through the living-room windows would sometimes get caught by it, refracted into a prism of colors on the wall. I liked the feel of it. Its coolness and heft, the smoothness of its sides.

The four of us kids were in bed that night. I shared a room with my younger brother. My two sisters were in their room upstairs in the attic. Our parents were outside at a block party. As I drifted off to sleep, I listened to the sounds of laughter and shouting rising in waves above the music.

When I remember that night, I see it all. I see everything that happened as if a movie is playing in my head. Yet I saw none of it. I heard it all, but I did not see any of what happened. I never left my bed.

Dad comes home first, slamming the front door and waking me. I hear him go into the kitchen and open the refrigerator, then the pop and hiss of a can of beer. He sits down in the living room, muttering to himself.

I see him in an oversized sombrero, a thin mustache penciled on his upper lip, bandoleers crossing his chest, and six-shooters at his sides. It is a costume party, and he is dressed as a Mexican bandit.

My mother comes to the front door and knocks. Dad doesn't get up. She knocks again, louder this time. "John, open the door." Dad sits, not moving. He is laughing.

She is now pounding on the door as my father's laughter grows. She rings the doorbell and then leans on it. The loud buzzer reverberates through the house. He just laughs louder.

My mother is screaming for him to let her in and banging on the door with her fists. My father turns on the TV. For a while it is quiet except for the muted sounds of the television.

Some time later there is a gentle knock.

"John, please open the door. It's very late."

It's Grandpa, Dad's father; Mom must have called him from a neighbor's house. "Oh, Christ," Dad mumbles as he gets up and opens the door.

I see my grandfather standing on the porch, looking at his bandito son, then down at the ground. Without saying another word, he turns and hurries down the porch steps.

After he leaves, my parents start in on each other. Dad staggers upstairs as Mom continues yelling. When he gets to the top, right outside my bedroom door, he turns to see my mother at the bottom of the stairs, holding the ashtray. She is dressed as a Dutch girl, wearing a triangular hat and false braids, rouge on her cheeks.

She surprises him by heaving the ashtray all the way up. He just manages to get out of the way as it hits the wall and thuds onto the floor. Still laughing, Dad picks up the ashtray and throws it back down. It hits the floor at the bottom of the stairs, careening into the closet door.

She throws it again, and he tosses it back, sending it tumbling down the stairs. They hurl it back and forth until both of them are spent.

My mother stays in the living room, smoking cigarettes. I can see her on the couch, the room blue with smoke, her hand shaking as she crushes another lipstick-stained Salem into the glass ashtray.

Many years later I asked my mother about that night.

"Of course I remember," she said. "I was locked out of my own house and not one of my four children would come down to let me in."

Daphne Gregory-Thomas

Daphne Gregory-Thomas spent forty-five years living and working as a high school educator in New Jersey and New York. Shortly after retiring from the classroom and writing many school reports, she discovered her new writing heartbeat by participating in the Memorial Sloan Kettering Visible Ink Writing Program. Her essays have been published in the *MSK Visible Ink Anthology* and by Zibby Media. They have also been performed at the annual MSK Visible Ink event, at *Writers Read*, and at the Yarmouth (Maine) Historical Society's Rooted Narratives event. She now resides in Kennebunk, Maine, and is an active member of Maine Writers and Publishers Alliance. Ever the essayist, she is also working on a long-form memoir project.

It Must Be the Wine

Daphne Gregory-Thomas

Weary in the airport, I wheel my suitcase toward check-in. Our well-planned trip to Athens, Santorini, and Mykonos is ending. We share a final toast with our traveling companions, a fine Greek wine from the airport bar.

My husband bends to whisper: “Let’s not leave.”

He approaches the ticket desk, asks what it will cost to change our return flight.

I stand speechless, confused.

“What are you doing?”

“We’re not leaving. I want to find our family.”

We’ve both grown up hearing stories of “the Mani,” the land of our common Spartan ancestors: tales of its rugged beauty, the fierce, loyal nature of the people, the famous vendettas, starting as far back as Achilles. We know we still have family there.

My husband is spontaneous, determined. I’m a teacher, structured, organized.

“We have tickets,” I protest. “Our family is expecting us back home. It must be the wine!”

“That’s exactly my point,” he claims. “The wine reminded me. Our family *is* waiting. We *are* going home.”

At that, our unplanned odyssey begins.

We rent a car, purchase maps, and end up in Gythio, the small harbor town that opens up to the high mountain roads of Mani and our family’s villages. In his best broken Greek, my husband asks a woman sweeping the sidewalk if she knows a name: *Demetroulakos*. The broom stops midair. “My name,” she cries, welcoming us with big Greek hugs and her homemade wine to celebrate our meeting. She hands us a bottle to take, no label or date, the vintage her indelible connection to my husband.

We continue up tiny roads to villages that hold promise of more relatives, ask a man walking a dog of my family. He gestures toward a hill with a vendetta lookout tower. We wind up dangerous switchbacks to a small cottage, pull a string that rings a bell. A wrinkled man in a funny hat emerges. "Boucouvalas," I announce. Again, spontaneous hugs encircle us, tears wet our cheeks. He too brings wine, fills our glasses, shows grainy pictures of family, many with the piercing blue eyes of my grandfather, who found his way to America as a boy, alone. This wine holds the taste of the hard times and history of those who left and those who stayed behind.

We drive on, see a man digging a ditch, say the name *Papaspryidakos*. He points to a house overlooking the sea. We find an open porch full of people, say the name again. They rush to hold us close. Platters of food fill the table next to jugs of wine made, we're told, from the grapes of my ancestors.

A withered uncle grabs his walking stick, points to the mountain.

"Now we go!"

We climb up hardscrabble paths through twisted groves of olive trees, then farther to an arbor laden with grapes, ripe and hanging low on the vines. Finally, an opening and an old stone house, the year 1886 etched by the door. Inside, on a crumbling wall, hangs a picture of my great grandparents.

"This their home," he proclaims. "We keep to remember."

It is one big room with a fireplace for cooking, a stone wheel for crushing olives into oil, a huge wooden vat where grapes were transformed into the wine of my lineage. In the corner, clay jugs hold the same wine my weathered uncle continues to ferment in honor of our ancestors, many forced to flee from war and starvation.

He fills our glasses. We quietly sip the wine of our history and all the stories it has to tell.

It's the sweetest wine I've ever tasted.

I touch the thin gold band that encircles my finger, once encircling the finger of my grandmother, who, as a young girl, lived in this old stone house before setting sail at fifteen, never to return.

At that moment, I know I've returned for her. I feel her deep in my blood and bones, her spirit and that of all the others who inhabited this place infused in the wine of my heritage, their legacy embodied in its vintage.

"It must be the wine," I say again, my palate savoring the memory waiting to be found on this mountain in Mani.

I have, indeed, come home to a family that has been expecting me, a glass of wine at the ready, and I thank my spontaneous, determined husband for knowing.

Mihai Grünfeld

Mihai Grünfeld was born in Cluj, Romania, where he lived until he was eighteen. In January 1969 he traveled to Czechoslovakia. This was the beginning of a long journey that took him to Israel, Italy, Sweden, and Canada in search of a home in the West. Eventually he settled in the U.S. He obtained his PhD from UC Berkeley and recently retired from Vassar College, where he taught Spanish and Latin American literature. Mihai's autobiography, *Leaving—Memories of Romania*, was published in 2008. Together with Sarah Levine Simon, he adapted his novel into a play entitled *The Dressmaker's Secret*, which enjoyed a successful run in New York City.

The Gift

Mihai Grünfeld

Once—only once—did my mother open the locks of her memory to tell me a story about Auschwitz. I was ten, and it happened quite unexpectedly, like a precious gift.

A Sunday morning, after breakfast, I was on my way outside to play when I heard Mama's voice from the bedroom. "Misike, come here."

She is sitting on the carpet, leaning against the wall with a soft pillow behind her back, holding a notebook on her lap.

"Sit down here with me. I want to teach you the Hebrew alphabet."

"Now?"

"Please, come and sit."

Bright sunlight pours in through the windows in front of me, lighting up the white crumpled sheets of my parents' unmade beds. Through the open windows I see the tops of the chestnut trees. Mama puts her arm around my shoulders and gently draws me close to her. I feel her warm arm against my skin and snuggle in. She opens the notebook and draws a few strange letters. These letters don't mean much to me, so I ask:

"Mama, would you tell me something about the concentration camps?"

As if waiting for something, she remains quiet. I don't dare move. The warm sunlight pours in through the open windows. Mama puts the notebook on the carpet and pulls me even closer. The morning air feels still around me. I can barely hear her soft dreamy voice despite the perfect stillness, and I don't dare look at her, afraid that she will stop.

"I was taken to Auschwitz during the summer of 1944 and spent the winter in a wooden barrack without any warm clothes. During the day, I worked in a factory, a long way from the barracks. I was hungry all the time."

A faint smile appears on Mama's face as she continues. "I was so hungry that I risked my life to get a bit of extra food."

Mama's voice perks up a little. "One night I got up and sneaked out of the barrack. I walked a few steps toward the fence that surrounded our camp, and then I crawled so the guards in the high posts wouldn't see me. A friend had told me about a spot where, through a hole under the barbed-wire fence, I could get out."

"What if the guards saw you?"

"They would have shot me, but I didn't care. I crept slowly into the field by the camp. It was early winter. I started digging the half-frozen ground with my fingers and eventually found a potato. I wiped it clean on my uniform and bit into it. As the piece warmed in my mouth, I chewed. It tasted really good, and I kept it in my mouth for a long time, before I swallowed."

At this moment Mama turns toward me with a faint smile. "Have you ever tasted a raw potato?"

"No."

She stands up, walks to the pantry and returns with a small potato and a knife. She sits down by me and slowly peels the potato, lost in her thoughts, so solemn I don't dare whisper a word. Then she cuts a thin slice and puts it in her mouth. She also cuts me a small piece. It tastes starchy to me, mostly bland and raw. I look at Mama's face as she eats it, very slowly. I expect her to cry, but she doesn't. She is somewhere else, far away.

"That potato tasted so good," she says, "I promised myself that, if I survived and ever got out, I would eat one raw potato every day."

I look at Mama: "Have you been eating a raw potato every day?"

"No, of course not," she says softly. "I don't want to remember anymore what happened there."

I snuggle up to her warm and soft body, hide my tears under her arm, and we remain quiet, looking out the window.

Manuela Hoelterhoff

Manuela Hoelterhoff is a commentator and editor whose topics have ranged widely over the contemporary world to include opera and theater, art and architecture, literature and travel, and how animals affect our lives. Her first articles appeared in William F. Buckley's *National Review*. There followed a twenty-year stint at *The Wall Street Journal*, where she wrote reviews and served as arts editor, books editor, and member of the editorial board and where she won the annual Pulitzer Prize for Criticism for her work, citing "her wide-ranging criticism on the arts and other subjects." A founding editor of *SmartMoney* magazine, she worked with Harold Evans on creating *Conde Nast Traveler.* Most recently, she served as an executive editor and columnist for *Bloomberg News* and was named a Guggenheim Fellow for her forthcoming book, Hitler's *Summer Seasons*.

Mugzie

Manuela Hoelterhoff

Mystery surrounded Mugzie from the day she arrived on the Upper West Side, tumbling out of a van dispatched by a sweet woman from a Brooklyn kill shelter after my friend Sheila and I got hopelessly lost trying to pick her up on an evening so stormy I wrote a poem about it.

Nothing was known about Mugzie except that a young dude had dropped her off saying his grandmother had died and no one wanted her. By contrast, the life of Mugzie's predecessor, the sainted Sugar, was well-documented since she had worked as a sniffer in the Beagle Brigade of the Department of Agriculture at Kennedy airport. Sugar's job was to separate illicitly imported meat products from tourists who feared this country might not have the perfect pepperoni. Sniffer dogs are trained to sit down in front of a suspicious suitcase; the handler rewards them with a treat.

After a sterling start, Sugar started sitting down in front of every suitcase.

Rendered useless by her greed, her employment came to an end, but the world became her oyster. She traveled widely and became known for her nocturnal escapes in Santa Fe, her heedless destructiveness (wreaked on any interfering curtains and windows) and guile (stealing anything off the plates of divas as they sat on the couch and reminisced about the past, oblivious to her lack of interest in anything not food related).

In contrast, Mugzie's prospects had seemed quite poor. The unbelievably sad picture of her on Petfinder.com showed a swaybacked dog seductively described as "senior and obese." Believed to be ten, she remained about that age, looking younger as her health improved. We spent six years together. She immediately took to the Sugar memorial bed by the fireplace.

Inspired by her soulful, searching eyes, we made up biographies for Mugzie. That name! And those huge front paws with crooked nails suggested a home without much of a lawn, but maybe a concrete patio where she shared in family barbecues. I couldn't help noticing that she always did her business on the flagstone at my house, never mind the acres of greenery available.

Unlike my other beagles, Mugzie loved fruits, vegetables, fish, even caviar on very special occasions. Perhaps an ancient Russian princess living in a draped apartment in Brighton Beach, our local Odessa not far from the shelter, had fed her tsarist scraps like scrumptious beets until she joined the Romanovs?

She was not a cuddler. Mugzie hated being picked up. Approach her and she would instantly roll on her back and show her belly while producing anguished shrieks. Maybe a defense mechanism from Sunday afternoons when the Russki princess's great-grandchildren came to visit.

Mugzie was friendly without being effusive and would trot over to favorite visitors like Miss Reller, provider of specially concocted frozen pup-cakes. Had she ever had pups? The only maternal instincts she revealed were for Minnie, another rescued beagle, who was possibly her age and got her face licked every morning.

When Hamlette the micro-pig arrived, Mugzie allowed her to share her bed, but looked the other way as dogs do to make annoying creatures disappear (out of sight, out of mind, and hopefully dead soon).

In 2008 we were both diagnosed with cancer. Her surgery cost more and wasn't covered. I laughed about that, but worried her days were numbered. Instead, we shared these happy last years. Mugzie was lying on her favorite suede bed as we shared our last salami sandwich. And she died while we were listening to Schubert's *Winterreise*. It seemed appropriate. These songs are about journeys—through Germany in the early nineteenth century and, in a larger sense, through a wintry world in which the narrator finds no shelter at sundown.

There are twenty-four songs, all settings of poems by Wilhelm Muller, another short-lived contemporary, starting with "Gute Nacht" and its hypnotic opening lines: "I was a stranger when I arrived, and a stranger when I left," sings the narrator as he quietly closes the door on a doomed love affair and leaves with the moonlight as his companion.

Winterreise has several references to dogs, who growl at the wanderer, the lonely outsider. My Mugzie never growled at anyone. There was always the possibility of a treat.

Margie Smith Holt

Margie Smith Holt is a Philly girl who fell in love with New York City as a student at NYU. She finally made it back twenty-five years later when she met an Upper West Sider and convinced him to marry her. In between, she had an Emmy-winning television career in Philadelphia, waitressed in the U.S. Virgin Islands, and sailed across the Atlantic in a thirty-foot boat. Today she owns a writing business and recently published her first book, *Not on Any Map: One Virgin Island, Two Catastrophic Hurricanes, and the True Meaning of Paradise.* She's also a volunteer mentor with the Visible Ink writing program for cancer patients at Memorial Sloan Kettering.

Wherever You Go, There You Are

Margie Smith Holt

The blow knocked the wind out of me.

I was flailing in the blue waters of the Virgin Islands, next to a sailboat that had capsized. With me on it. I needed to get the boat upright, pushed with all my might on the centerboard for leverage.

It wouldn't budge.

The sailing instructor—floating calmly, watching me struggle—righted the boat, with no help from me, and we clambered back on.

"Did you get hit in the head with the boom?" she asked.

"Yes," I sputtered.

"Hard?"

"Yes."

"Get used to it."

Back on land I dumped a gallon of fresh water from a plastic jug over my head, wriggled into dry clothes right there in the parking lot, and raced to a burger shack called Skinny Legs where I was a "waitress" in much the same way I was a "sailor."

What the hell was I thinking?

I had been on television in Philadelphia. A star reporter! Always camera ready.

There was proof, even in the remote tropical outpost I now called home. A bartender had discovered one of my old eight-by-ten glossy headshots and tacked it up over the cash register, "MANAGER ON DUTY" scrawled underneath.

"Hey!" said my boss, genuinely surprised, when he saw the publicity photo. "You used to be on TV?"

His newest waitress didn't look like she even owned a mirror.

I had ditched makeup. Couldn't find my blow-dryer. The last guy to cut my hair delivered beach snacks from a powerboat.

My journalism career—which I loved—had ended abruptly three years earlier. I was forced out for—take your pick: Too old? Too expensive? Too mouthy? Today you'd get a lawyer. Back then you just moved on.

Next came a PR gig. Not a passion, but a steady paycheck, better hours. Perfect since I wanted to get married and have kids.

When that blew up too, I did exactly what no practical rule-follower ever dreams of doing: Quit my job. Sold my car. Bought a one-way ticket to the Caribbean.

"What are you going to do?" sneered the ex. "Swab the decks?"

I didn't know. Maybe.

"Is this some kind of a mid-life crisis or something?" asked one of the millennials at work.

I was about to turn forty, so . . . hard to argue with the math.

I moved with no plan, vowed to do nothing resembling my old life, but the local newspaper editor—or was it my old life?—stalked me, tricked me into writing.

Instead of presidents, I interviewed pirates.

"Wherever you go, there you are!" a T-shirt hanging in the Jolly Dog souvenir shop taunted.

Being an island "reporter" had its perks. I wore flip-flops and "researched" over rum cocktails. At long last, a chance to test my theory that a glass of wine or two might make me a better writer! I interviewed Santa Claus—off duty—at the bar. Santa drank vodka soda with a splash of cranberry.

"How's your daughter doing down there?" relatives asked my mother. "Has she found herself yet?"

"I don't think she's looking," she replied.

"How are you really doing?" my friends wrote. "Have you changed?"

"Yes!" I'd say. "I look like I did when we were thirteen!"

Like when we were girls, planning our lives.

"Was it hard to make such a drastic leap?" people asked. They mean the change of address, but harder, by far, was the career change. I had defined myself by what I did: reporter. Who was I without the title?

I did finally learn to sail.

I sailed across the Atlantic in a thirty-foot boat with no engine and a bucket for a bathroom. It was an epic adventure.

And later, when back-to-back hurricanes destroyed the paradise that shaped my future, I covered the story.

Twenty years since that life-changing move, I'm a different person. Still a journalist. More myself than ever.

Sally G. Hoskins

Sally G. Hoskins is a retired college biology professor formerly employed at City College of the City University of New York, where she developed the CREATE project, aimed at transforming the teaching and learning of biology through a focus on close reading of primary literature (peer-reviewed research reports) rather than textbooks. She also founded and conducted SHE, a women's vocal ensemble (1998–2005) that gave free concerts and raised funds for NYC-based charitable organizations through voluntary donations. Her essays have appeared in *The New York Times, Newsweek,* and *Science,* as well as in anthologies from the Visible Ink project and *Writers Read.*

Not as Expected

Sally G. Hoskins

How writing my first book got me through the pandemic

As a biologist, my initial reaction to the pandemic was, *Science will get us out of this*, followed closely by, *People will soon understand and respect laboratory research much more*. I was half right.

I'm a retired college professor, living in a tiny cottage in Putnam County, where, during our pandemic summer I coped by trying to grow flowers from seed, taking long walks, and catching up on sitcoms I missed during graduate school. In a June phone session with my longtime psychiatrist, I rambled—again—about "someday" compiling the essays I'd produced in recreational writing classes into a book. This time, she said, "Why not self-publish?"

Feeling unmoored that day, I heard the suggestion as a command. I dug into my files and unearthed drafts of some seventy essays marked up years ago by writing-group classmates, then spent the summer rewriting fifty of them, appreciative of every praised turn of phrase, correction of misused semicolons, or marginal "LMAO." By September, I had a complete draft of "the book," though I learned that, as with grant proposals for the National Science Foundation, you're not done when it's written. Grants need Budget Justifications, Facilities Statements, and BioSketches. A self-published book involves decisions on issues I'd never considered: dimensions, fonts, drop caps, headers, and paper stock. The only easy part was the title—*Not as Expected*—the box I'd checked on more than one Lands' End "Reason for Return" form. It was an all-purpose excuse for rejecting something without having to explain how your expectations misaligned with reality. The title essay focused on the year I became an instant single mother to my orphaned teenage niece. For her, it was time to rebel against nonexistent parents. I, in contrast, was thinking Daughter I Never Had, or at least Gilmore Gal-Pal. Hijinks ensued.

I chose a book-publishing crew from Ohio since I'm originally a Midwesterner. Their guidance helped until we got to cover design—another Not as Expected experience. They proposed taking that chore off my hands—for five hundred dollars. Uh, no. I would do my own cover. It looked easier than parenting. I plucked a pink zinnia I'd personally germinated, photographed it emerging from an eggshell, then mastered a minimal InDesign skillset. Even though it took me half a day to figure out how to draw a frame around the photo, doing everything myself was undeniably satisfying.

I first sent the finished compilation to very close friends, a super-supportive fan base. Then I expanded to a wider circle: former teachers, an ex, several once-dear but now distant friends. I dithered over sending a copy to a revered senior colleague, as we'd had a bumpy three-decade relationship. Finally, however, I mailed it, then panicked on the way home from the post office.

A week later I received an email from her with high praise and "thanks for the guffaws." She also recounted a heartfelt tale of fraught interactions with a teenager who unexpectedly joined her household, which she reflected on after reading my version. Her sincere, revealing email was heartening. I was glad I had taken the risk.

I've been okay during the pandemic because I'm a hermit at heart and because my retirement preceded Zoom's takeover of academia. Even as I have turned inward, though, my book has allowed me to reveal myself in a candid and meaningful way. My essays range from ruminating on why the world of Thomas the Tank Engine is 95 percent male, to wondering whether I could get rich quick by following the well-established formula for writing summer-on-Nantucket chick lit, to pieces about coping with chronic illness. One essay reveals a close call with suicidal ideation. In conversation, I'm not sure I would have ever gone there, even with old friends. Writing made it easier. My readers' wide-ranging reactions have been Not as Expected, different than expected, often deeper than expected. We're closer now. And I've learned to expect more, of myself.

Isaiah Hunt

Born and raised as a proud Cleveland native, **Isaiah Hunt** focuses on near-future stories of his community, the entertainment industry, and transhumanist capitalism. When he's not fiddling around with music, or studying Pan-African history, he's daydreaming of worlds adjacent to our own. He has recently finished his MFA in creative writing and is a Hopkins Fellow for John Carroll University, where he currently teaches fiction writing. His work can be found at the Wick Poetry Center, *Luna Negra, On The Run*, and elsewhere.

My Stories, My Metallurgy

Isaiah Hunt

My ancestors were superheroes off the coasts of West Africa who maintained a ritual kinship with rock and ore. The Igbo, Earth's first iron men, flourished within their forges. The strikes of a blacksmith's *otutu* onto their *ihuama* were akin to drum patterns used to invoke their supreme being, Chukwu, for protection as strong as steel.

However, any metal unprayed for is an Igbo's kryptonite.

Colonization brought ships full of shackles and chains enchanted with unholy power to shatter families and untether traditions. Thousands of Igbo tossed themselves overboard to return their souls home. My ancestors endured the harsh voyage. I imagine my ancestors arriving in Virginia from the Calvin Presley slave ship, hearing the lands, too, pleading for salvation.

Probably why my great-great-grandfather chose to be a vigilante in the depths of Alabama. He wasn't a perfect man, poisoned by alcohol and the remnants of slavery. Some might call him a murderer. Others, a hero.

Regardless, the incident might've happened at a bar where a white man must've baited him with slurs and threats, and my great-great-grandfather clutched the hilt of his knife or gripped the metal of his gun, like gums to a tooth. I'd imagine the anger of my ancestors charged that bullet, or ignited the fury within the knife, its sharp iron tip whispering, "I hear you."

Avoiding nooses and burning crosses to flee north with his family, he permitted my great-grandmother to step outside of her house, the first Black family in East Cleveland, Ohio, to sip the stable suburban life.

One of her daughters was my grandmother, blessed with skin as beautiful and brown as the wood my ancestors blessed before burning it into charcoal. She met a man at a carnival whose voice was as warm and electrifying as sparks from an anvil. I imagine them two hundred feet high on a Ferris wheel—the closest my blood has reached for the stars, farthest from the threats of a white man's tongue—dreaming of life's next destination.

That all changed when he won the lottery.

Congratulations, it's time to serve your country.

His reward? An M1 carbine and a free ticket to a land thick with rice fields, Agent Orange, and the supposed communism that antagonizes the American Dream. Even my ancestors could not shield him from witnessing the worst of humanity. He left as a malleable man of steel, returning a broken veteran.

His final reward was an asylum, where a pipe bomb finished what war could not.

And my mother, a decade under the sun, listened intently in her classroom as the teacher nonchalantly read off each victim's name on the morning newspaper as if it were a simple shopping list. My mother didn't raise her hand. She did not cry. Calmly, she laid her no. 2 pencil down, approached the teacher, and whispered, "That's my father."

When her mother, too, was prepared to meet death—doctors predicted a couple of months—my mother's powers had awoken. She invoked Chukwu within her DNA, praying over the tubes and ports of the tomotherapy machine to negate the poison festering in her mother's flesh. She was not ready to lose another. When doctors found no trace of my grandmother's cancer, they attributed it to a miracle.

While I'm not gifted with the abilities to smith, protect, or heal, my mother passed down the stories she wished to tell the world but instead whispered to me within her womb during starry nights. Thus, I was born bearing that same fascination for metal as my ancestors. My stories about Black astronauts piercing skies with spaceships, and Black musicians bending their instruments to orchestrate new music, is my hammer to the anvil. My words, reconnected with the forgotten. I am the reparations of Igbo ancestors lost to colonization, slavery, and time. My pencil is my *otutu*. The page, my *ihuama*. My stories, my metallurgy.

Marilyn Ogus Katz

Marilyn Ogus Katz taught in an educational opportunity program at SUNY Purchase and then served as dean of studies at Sarah Lawrence College. She left academia to write, primarily fiction. She completed a novel, *The Old City*, about a family of Latvian Jews caught between Hitler and Stalin, and her collection of linked short stories, *A Few Small Stones*, about coming of age in an extended immigrant family, was published in 2018. Essays on Wordsworth, teaching writing, issues in higher education, and the concerns of older women have appeared in journals and anthologies. Marilyn once said, "As a late bloomer, I have to believe, along with Grace Paley, in 'Enormous Changes at the Last Minute.'"

A Few Small Stones

Marilyn Ogus Katz

My cousin Harvey only calls when there's a death in the family. He's the custodian of our cemetery plot and must ask them to "open the grave," as though beneath the deceptive lid of grass, an empty space lies waiting.

Cousin Florence has died of a heart attack. Once again, Harvey suggests we drive out together. We haven't seen each other since the last funeral. But over sixty years earlier, I babysat him as he toddled about, blond ringlets at his neck. Each mile on the Long Island Expressway takes us back to the past we share.

We grew up in that cemetery. Some families take pride in a homestead or a compound on a river. Ours struggled to preserve a patch of burial ground. In the 1930s, our grandmother and her five younger siblings, immigrants from Poland, bought a plot with sixty graves. They insisted we Jews own a piece of land from which no one could turn us away.

The family met on the first Saturday of each month in someone's home. Even as a child I understood the difference between an uncle and a great-uncle, a second cousin and a first cousin once removed. My grandmother held forth, her gold watch swinging like a pendulum below her waist. Bubbe, a leader at the Workmen's Circle, could keep an agenda even in a room of boisterous brothers and sisters. Maintaining the cemetery plot was the first item of business, but the family also sent money to a sister in Poland, raised funds for the poor, planned the Hanukkah party and the annual picnic. Bubbe embraced the democracy of her adopted country and encouraged debate, but she always got her way.

We children fell asleep, snuggling among the abandoned coats on the bed, awakening overheated, and staggering into the night with imprints of coat buttons on our cheeks. When the great-uncles and great-aunts died, I visited our plot again and again, as easy around the gravestones as on the swings at the state park where we went for our picnics.

Harvey clutches the wheel and peers into the rain. I'm glad I brought my umbrella. His wife, Cynthia, died eleven years earlier; my husband, Mac, twenty. In the Jewish tradition, we will place small stones on their footstones today.

"What's with this strictly funeral relationship we have?" I say. "When I go, you'll have to introduce yourself and your children to mine."

"You were the best babysitter," Harvey says. "Remember that New Year's when we leaned out the window and banged pans against the sill?" But he doesn't promise to call between deaths.

We drive through the cemetery gates toward a dense skyline of monuments, so unlike the lawns of our childhood. When we step into the downpour, I don't recognize anyone except the husband of the cousin who died. We are a small family above ground.

The rabbi asks us to place a shovelful on the casket. The soil is drenched and heavy, the shovel hard to lift and turn. The thud and scatter of pebbles assaults the pine box again and again. When I bend to place the stone on my husband's grave, I long to laugh with him once more about these relatives who argued every month, as they reached for roast chicken and potato kugel, about what shrubs to plant at the cemetery.

Now only Harvey and I remember the aunt who knit sweaters with armholes too tight to move, the great-uncle who paid for my mother's piano lessons, the cousin who ground gefilte fish each Passover, or Bubbe, who marched to demand the vote for women. Soon our family's cherished plot will fill with distant relatives who won't know or care about that once vibrant community of immigrants.

And Harvey will pull away from my corner with my drenched old umbrella on the floor of his car.

Hunter Klein

Hunter Klein is a Brooklyn-based writer, producer, teacher, improviser, former little league umpire, and hopelessly romantic New York Jets supporter. After graduating from the University of Pennsylvania with a degree in economics, Hunter realized he knew virtually nothing about economics, so he pursued his other passions—teaching, writing, and comedy. With compatriots at the Upright Citizens Brigade Theater and the People's Improv Theater, he's performed throughout New York City and recently wrote, directed, and acted in a musical fiction podcast series entitled *The Story of Heidelberg*, which earned him a Silver Award at the National Audio Theater Festival. Hunter's next audio series, slated for release next year, follows a pair of vigilante crime fighters in the 1950s who are bad at their jobs.

Tennis Shoes

Hunter Klein

When I was eight years old, my friend Jacob was over at my house to play video games on the third floor. Significantly, the third floor was also the abode of my grandparents that week—in from Florida, my unfettered grandmother could stretch her legs up there, while my no-nonsense grandfather could cozy up with a book and nap, undeterred by the ululations of a house of four kids under ten. Quiet. Except, of course, for Jacob and me.

I don't remember if he asked us to go downstairs—I was too rapt in our game, craning around him to maintain position—but I do remember Jacob's face when Pop-Pop shrugged, unbothered, and promptly removed all his clothes, cap to crocs, and sat on the couch beside us.

Thus was my friend's introduction to my nudist grandparents.

They weren't religious nudists. More cultural, in the way we're cultural Jews, or even cultural bowlers. We don't practice much, but we love the community and vibes. They wouldn't "observe" in public—no, my grandfather would don his typical cologne-soaked pressed polo, his gold watch obscuring the black panther tattoo inked during his stint in prison, and his trusty WWE hat. Back in the confines of their Florida home, though, all "bets" were off. On the couch, on the floor, on the mind of my poor mother.

"It's insane, Stu!" she'd lament of her in-laws. "Your mother just said she got back from a weeklong cruise, where they packed nothing but their tennis shoes." Of course, her concerns lay not in her own fears, her own peripheral glimpse of bonus extremities, but ours. Which is fair. Not only were we getting constant exposure, but, worse in her mind, we were acclimating. Opening. And soon enough, to a certain extent, in the confines of our home, with the notable exception of my scarred little sister . . . we were practicing. To my mother's chagrin and grandmother's unmitigated delight, clothes were no longer a part of the fabric of this family.

Even my grandfather, in all respects a stern man, a jukebox of moral impartations, would be tickled at stories of nine-year-old me violating the dress code at the golf course for wearing jeans, and then violating it again later when the jeans came off. Between lectures on reading and excuses—"no breaks" his patented slogan—he'd take us to movies with topless women and bottomless men.

My father's stepdad, my grandfather would often remark about the love in our family, the openness, the importance of being open. How discouragement and rebuke would, say, do my speech-delayed younger brother more harm than good. Welcomeness, tolerance, nakedness—these were things my therapist mother could get behind.

Our nudity levels declined as we got older, and unfortunately, so did our grandparents'. Over the years, Pop-Pop was diagnosed with dementia, and he passed in 2021. We reflected on the laundry list of lessons he left us, but my mom in particular noted how much she loved him for his actions, the role he played and the hole he'd leave as a father and grandfather. It was true—I'd gotten his WWE hat, but I missed him.

Just a few months earlier, we visited my younger brother studying in Berlin. Now fully, unabashedly, unapologetically himself, he opted to take us—myself, my parents, and my girlfriend—to a "bathhouse he'd heard of," unaware of the full extent of their "textile-free" policy. It was mortifying.

My girlfriend stayed with my mom, eyes wired shut, dodging stray droops and sags like a special op, cemented to the lone pool where clothing was permitted, while my brother, my father, and I sat in our mandated skin-suits, Dad cracking jokes with some new friends. The German in charge shushed him up—this was a silent naked sauna. There would be no laughter here.

Except, of course, from my grandfather, undoubtedly smiling down, in just his tennis shoes.

Beth Kwon

Beth Kwon is a writer and editor based in New York City; she has served as a communications director at Columbia University and Barnard College and is currently a speechwriter at NYU. A former journalist, she was an editor and writer at *Women's Wear Daily* and *Newsweek*, and her work has appeared in *Allure, Time Out New York, The Village Voice,* and *Fortune*, among other outlets. Beth also publishes a personal zine, called BKNY.

Lucky Baby

Beth Kwon

I had my second child when I was forty-one, and due to my age, I was a "geriatric" mother, as my obstetrician frequently reminded me. (I chose him for his experience and proximity to my office, not for his tact.) But I had read enough WebMD articles to know there were risks, and I felt fortunate that I had been able to conceive. While I was expecting, I picked up every lucky penny I spotted.

There are many abandoned pennies to be found in New York City. I found the talismans on the sidewalk, on the subway, on stairwells, in elevators. I found them when it was sunny, rainy, snowy, and in puddles, piles of leaves, or on manholes. They were sometimes shiny, dingy, or downright filthy. I only claimed them if they were heads up, of course. During the nine months I carried my daughter, I amassed 124 pennies, which I still keep on a bookshelf in my bedroom.

I'm not sure how I became so superstitious. Perhaps I got it from my paternal grandmother. She believed eating the small, mostly meatless tip of a chicken wing would invite misfortune. She was also convinced that my middle name was bad luck. In Korean culture, a person's name often carries a character denoting which generation you belong to—but it's traditionally bestowed to males. My father had three daughters and no sons, so he gave us the character Yong in our Korean middle names, which indicates we belong to the thirty-eighth generation of our family name, Kwon. My grandmother promptly gave us her own new names, insisting that because we are girls, the names assigned by our father were bad luck.

I collected the pennies even though I knew many mothers who were older than me who had had healthy births. I knew the chances of my pregnancy going awry were relatively slim.

But there is a sort of anxiety-fueled curriculum to modern pregnancy that one can get caught up in. Don't consume sushi, cold cuts, or wine. Exercise just enough, but not too much. Listen to classical music. Avoid stress. It's a long nine months of trying to live your healthiest life for another creature's future. In spite of the odds in my favor, it felt like a gamble.

There were a few bumps: During my second trimester, a scan showed my baby had a short femur, which could be a sign of a genetic defect. I developed gestational diabetes, prompting my doctor to strap me to a machine twice a week to monitor my vitals. I am fortunate these were the only issues I encountered.

My baby was due in early September, and by the end of summer, I was ready to stop lumbering around. Besides, it was becoming trickier to bend down and pick up coins. I began to curse New Yorkers who were so careless with their change, but I felt that if I ignored a found penny, it might somehow contribute to my daughter's downfall.

Two and a half weeks before her due date, I decided it was time. Before leaving work on a Friday, I told a colleague, "Beyonce's coming," referring to our nickname for my unborn girl. And that weekend, in what might be the first and last instance in which my daughter obeyed me without objection, my water broke, we headed to the hospital, and she soon arrived, safe and sound. We named her Nora.

My dad chose a Korean name for her: Kyung-Gu. Kyung means dignified, and Gu means nine, indicating she is of the thirty-ninth generation of the Kwon line, which can be traced to a single lineage. If superstition prevails, I'm not too concerned about misfortune that might come from bestowing the character on her even though she's a girl. She has a whole pile of lucky pennies to protect her.

Ann Levin

Ann Levin is a widely published writer and book reviewer. She enjoyed a long journalistic career at the Associated Press, covering elections as well as every imaginable natural and human disaster. Originally from western Pennsylvania, Ann traveled north to Smith College for her undergraduate studies, south to the University of Texas for her creative writing graduate degree, and finally opted for the East—that is, New York's Upper East Side, where she and her husband now live. Ann's work appears regularly in many journals. A small sampling includes *Sensitive Skin, Southeast Review, Potato Soup Journal,* and *Smoky Blue Literary and Arts Magazine.* She's also a frequent contributor to the New York–based writers group *Writers Read*. You can find her at annlevinwriter.com and follow her on Instagram and X @annlevinnyc.

The Majesty of Nature

Ann Levin

I parked in front of the ashram and turned to Annie B. "This is it," I said. "Our last chance to talk." Two hours earlier, we'd been sweltering in Boston traffic, choking on fumes. But for miles now, ever since we got off the Massachusetts Turnpike and onto the shady roads that led to the retreat, we hadn't seen a soul.

Inside the administration building a shaggy-haired man in faded overalls reviewed the rules. "No outside food, alcohol, sex, or drugs. Most of all, no talking," he said, tugging at his beard. "Here, we practice noble silence."

Annie B. had been on retreats before, even in India, but this was my first, and I was glad to have her along. She was my father's oldest sister, born not long after the turn of the twentieth century, a hippie before hippies, and a beatnik too. She smoked a little pot, listened to jazz, and during her long insomniac nights, played tapes of the Indian mystic Krishnamurti. Every spring, when snow was on the ground, she looked for lady slippers in the woods, and later in the season, for morels and ramps. Widowed at a young age, she had no shortage of admirers, in part because she was gorgeous: dark-complexioned, high cheekbones, a straight nose; a little like the Hindu goddess Parvati, if Parvati had been Jewish.

In our food- and health-crazed family, Annie B. was known for her buckwheat pancakes, brown rice casseroles, coq au vin—and headstands. She also walked backward on the high school track. When my mom invited her to dinner, she'd finish off the meal with five almonds for longevity and a gold-tipped Black Sobranie cigarette, just one a day because they tasted so good.

That summer in the Berkshires, I was fresh out of college, taking life very seriously; she was about seventy and wore her thick, gray-streaked hair in a fat braid down her back. When we got to our dorm rooms, I reminded her of the rules: "Remember, no talking."

"Right," she said solemnly, then burst into a gleeful cackle.

For the next week, our days were divided into walking and sitting meditations, with dharma lectures at night. Sitting quietly, doing nothing—it wasn't easy; my feet fell asleep, I couldn't sit up straight. Sometimes, I'd doze off and start to tip over. To avoid embarrassment, I'd head outside for walking meditation, to pace back and forth on a dirt path worn into the side of a hill.

One day, gazing out at the wooded slopes, I sensed the terrifying otherness of the pines. Majestic, yes; beautiful, absolutely; but also mute, inhuman, oblivious to my humdrum concerns. They weren't green either. They were bluish-green, verging on blue.

That night, outside our dorm rooms, I whispered to Annie B., "Out there, on the walking path, amid the majesty of nature. I think I got it, what Krishnamurti talks about . . . or maybe it's the Dalai Lama. You know: Emptiness! Nothingness! It was amazing!"

"Here, have a Hershey's bar," she said, pulling me into her room. "Celebrate your breakthrough!"

"Where did you get this?" I said, astonished.

"From that darling girl who's sleeping with the meditation instructor," she said.

"What?" I exclaimed. "How do you know that?"

"Because she told me. She told me all about these holy teachers, and let me tell you, they get around!"

It turned out that Annie B., despite the rule on noble silence, had been chatting up everyone since the day we got there. She even found a meditator who brought a stash of wine. Looking back, I realize just how much I learned from her. About the art of living. That you can find your bliss in a meditation hall or in the great outdoors, and you don't have to give up sex, drugs, chocolate, or booze.

Steven Lewis

Steve Lewis: husband-father-grandfather first, then, in short order, writer, mentor, editor, swinger of birches. His work has been published widely, from the notable to the beyond obscure, from *The New York Times* and *The Washington Post* to the *Road Apple Review*, including a biblically long list of parenting publications (seven kids, seventeen grandkids). His recent books include a novel, *The Lights Around the Shore*, and a poetry collection titled *Fire in Paradise*, coauthored with his daughter Elizabeth Bayou-Funk. Steve and his wife, Patti, live under the shadow of Bonticou Crag in New Paltz, New York.

Driving into Darkness

Steven Lewis

If memory serves me correctly, and even if it doesn't, Richard's mother would have packed enough Mott's apple juice, roast beef and turkey sandwiches, pears and apples, Oreo cookies, and paper napkins for the entire senior class at Wheatley High. But this was no class trip. And there were just four heedless boys piling into my 1956 Ford Fairlane at 11 p.m. on a cold November night.

Recently painted "British Racing Green" ($29.95 at Earl Scheib on Jericho Turnpike), the Fairlane was an underpowered, automatic-transmission junker with tan Naugahyde seats and a cracked dashboard. Something local dads would drive back and forth to the train station. What my father called a beater. For me it beat the hell out of taking the school bus . . . or hitching rides . . . or worse, being driven anywhere by my parents. It was freedom I had never before known.

I suspect Mr. Gaynor gathered us around the oval pine table in their Albertson dining room, unfolded his Rand McNally roadmap and showed us, inch by excruciating inch, the way: the LIE to the BQE to the Verrazzano-Narrows and across Staten Island to the Goethals Bridge and then the long Jersey Turnpike . . .

And aside from an unscheduled stop at the Joyce Cary Rest Area (so Jon, the most mechanical of this unmechanical crew, could jerry-rig the hanging, spark-spitting muffler), we headed straight down 95, rumbling through darkly industrial Baltimore at 3 a.m., arriving in DC an hour later.

The melancholy line of mourners under hazy streetlamps leading to the Rotunda was miles long. A cop on horseback looked at the heap, leaned over and peered in at us, shook his head, and said we'd never make it in time. Twisting around and pointing behind, he suggested we drive out to Arlington.

I have no idea how we found our way, but we drove through the cemetery gates before dawn, four boys shivering down into the dewy lawn.

We were there before the groundskeepers would place a carpet of fake grass around the dark rectangular hole. Before soldiers staked out their posts. Before Secret Service men in dark suits kicked us out of the low branches of a tree. Before the crowds of adults elbowed their way in front of us. Before the caissons . . . Nehru . . . Haile Selassie . . . Charles de Gaulle, his high hat high above the cold crowd.

It has always mystified me that our typically overprotective suburban parents had allowed us to leave our safe homes that evening. Four coddled boys with combined social IQs too low to pass the American history regents, piling into that green jalopy and heading out for a rendezvous with history.

In five years I would be married . . . in six years become a dad . . . crooning Kristofferson's cautionary words about freedom to my baby boy. Decades would pass before I would teach each of my seven teenagers to drive.

But some fifty-five years later, peering back through a lifetime of computer screens and windscreens, rumbling across endless highways and back roads, engines purring, engines failing, I know in my dad soul that there are no satisfying answers to the really important whys of this life.

And as a writer, I know that the story is not the story. The story is just a vehicle to drive us deeper into the unspoken real story.

As it is here, with only hazy context and lost time as a roadmap, this tale is not simply about four dumb boys attending a slain president's funeral. The real story is about the moment I gripped my fingers around the plastic steering wheel of that 1956 Ford with its grossly underpowered engine, its hideous paint job, and pressed the gas pedal to the floor . . . driving us into the night and those first dark truths about the inscrutable, unimaginable world we'd be entering.

Betty MacDonald

For almost forty years, storytelling has influenced **Betty MacDonald's** work, especially as a performer with Community Playback Theatre in the Hudson Valley. A versatile artist—writer, actor, and storyteller—she helped create and performed in TMI Project's *What to Expect When You're Not Expecting*. Currently, Betty hosts *Words Carry Us*, a monthly livestream event featuring readings and conversations with local writers and artists. Her essays and poems are anthologized in *80 Things to Do When You Turn 80, Open House, Better with Age,* and *Lightwood*. Betty is a longtime *Writers Read* contributor, delighting audiences with essays on topics including love, motherhood, and coming of age.

First Love

Betty MacDonald

Because he slips into her bed at night after he comes home from a date. Because he is insistent, she lets him. She lets him because she adores her brother with the intensity of a little sister. She knows it's wrong.

She longs for his approval. After years of ignoring her and putting her down, he's focused on her. He wants her. She wants to be special.

She tries to stop but the lure to please him overrides her resistance.

She stops him from "going all the way." They do everything else. Her boundaries battered and porous from her father's incessant assault . . . She wonders if her brother is also the object of unwanted touching from their father.

When she is nine and her brother thirteen, they are the same height. Their mother's nightmare: a shrimp of a son and a giant daughter. At eleven and fifteen they look like twins, twin nymphs. He is tall by then and handsome. They're so young, so fresh bodied, like star-crossed lovers . . . like loving brother and sister, god and goddess in a Greek myth, in a Celtic myth . . . in a Viking myth. So much alike, could you tell them apart when they were entwined in each other's arms?

On a visit to their uncle a few years later, their uncle remarks, "You act as if you are his wife, not his sister."

Is that just a snarky remark? Does he know?

Does he know her fantasy dreamlike, locked-away secret, not to be revealed, not to be acted upon: her lover, a male version of herself, her exact counterpart. No one can know.

Fortunately what they share is forbidden. Without that inhibition she would have lost herself in him.

On the one hand she is dragged down by the weight of the secret . . . the forbidden-ness of it.

On the other she loves the star-crossed-ness, love-that-can-never-be, tragic story of it. Willingly, she promises herself she will welcome letting go when he commits to someone else.

When it ends it has gone on for ten years.

They never speak about it. They don't even have a name for it. Later on she tells friends, therapists, a twelve-step group, anyone who will listen. He tells no one. He doesn't admit it to himself.

In his early sixties he is diagnosed with Alzheimer's. When she visits him at his nursing home he thinks it is 1950; he thinks they are in their teens.

On these rare visits they sit side by side, holding hands, saying little. She could say she feels their souls touching, she could say there is an electric current, but it's not like that. A powerful feeling like no other courses from his hand into hers. She weeps whenever she remembers the feeling of their hands pressed together.

He was mean when they were kids. He never forgave her for reducing his lofty, privileged only-child status to that of big brother. She had loved him unconditionally, in spite of his cutting her hair off, sawing her tricycle in half, burning the end of her nose with the cigarette lighter in the new Chevrolet. Her cousin asks, "Do you remember when he held you down with a pillow over your face till you passed out?" She doesn't.

At 78 the Alzheimer's has advanced. She is the only person he recognizes.

He has broken his hip. The hip has healed. But he can't walk. He's forgotten how. It's near the end.

She sits, pressing herself into him as close as she can. She holds his hand firmly. She wills the closeness to direct her words to what shreds of memory he has left.

"I forgive you," she says. "Do you understand?"

"Yes," he says, nodding. "I think I do!"

George Mannes

George Mannes moved to New York City long ago to make his fortune. He did not make his fortune—most likely because he ended up working as a journalist—but he stuck around anyway. George has a weakness for collecting things that no one else values, including souvenir airsickness bags and Do Not Disturb signs from hotels, and the two most prized books in his library are a rare copy of *Red Channels* and an original edition of *Weegee's Naked City*. George is executive editor of *AARP The Magazine* and the *AARP Bulletin*, the largest-circulation magazines in the United States.

My Left Foot

George Mannes

"How's your toe?" a neighbor asked me a few days ago.

"It's still missing," I said.

I got home, took off my running shoes and my socks, and lay on the bed. Yep, still only nine toes. If I press my bare feet together, ankle to ankle, there's an empty space where my left big toe should be. With all the other toes lined up together, I'm reminded of a smile with one of the front teeth knocked out.

I had fifty-nine good years with that toe. We were, in a word, inseparable. But then came December 7, 2021. I woke up that morning with ten toes. I went to sleep that night with nine.

I'd known for several weeks that this might happen. The blood blister I'd noticed on my toe in early September had turned out to be a ridiculously obscure form of melanoma, one that was potentially fatal. Part of the standard treatment, given how far the cancer had advanced, was to amputate the toe. So given the choice between living with nine toes and dying with ten, I chose nine. As I wrote in my diary, "Seems like a small price to pay."

A small price. I've spent the last two years wondering how small that price really was. Which I think is another way of saying, *Do I want sympathy? Do I deserve sympathy?* I go back and forth on this. Some of the things I feared at the outset haven't come true. I still have my balance. I still can go running, and I don't go around lopsided. I don't think anyone looks at me and says, *What's up with that guy?* In fact, when I've gone barefoot at the beach, I don't think anyone has noticed at all. One of my biggest worries was that my future grandchildren, if I ever have grandchildren, will be freaked out by Grandpa's missing toe. But then a friend of mine told me that when he was a kid, he thought his grandfather's missing finger was the coolest thing in the world.

Unlike the young man who fit me for my orthotic, who got too close to a lawnmower as a child, I didn't lose half my foot. I didn't lose my whole foot. I didn't lose a leg. It may be technically correct to call myself an amputee, but it doesn't feel morally right.

The upshot is that I don't deserve sympathy. And I don't want it. Most of the time, that is. Eventually, I'm going to run another marathon, and I have this fantasy about when I do. I'm going to get myself a T-shirt, and on the back it will say, "Ask me about acral lentiginous melanoma." And on the front it will say, "I only have nine toes." I want to tell people, *You may not realize this, but I'm injured. I look okay on the outside, but I'm suffering where you can't see.*

Whenever I bathe in this fantasy, I end up realizing, of course, that I'm no different from anyone else. Everyone I know in my life, everyone I pass on the street, we are all suffering inside, to a certain degree. We all have hidden injuries that most of the time we keep to ourselves, that other times we want the whole world to know about.

So this is how I've changed. My hurt, easy for other people to overlook, reminds me that we all have hurts that are easy for other people to overlook. As I slowly fall apart, I'm more aware that everyone else is too. I wish I didn't have to lose a toe to have a deeper understanding of other people's hidden pain. But we all have things we wish didn't happen to us. It's not like I'm special.

David Masello

David Masello moved to New York City from Evanston, Illinois, and has made his living as a writer and editor for more than forty years. He continually explores and discovers new things in the cityscape—some of which turn into the minute-long, self-narrated videos he posts on Instagram. David's career began as a nonfiction book editor at Simon & Schuster; he then held senior editorial positions at many magazines, including *Travel & Leisure, Art and Antiques,* and *Town and Country.* He's currently executive editor of *Milieu*, a magazine about design and architecture. A widely published essayist, poet, and playwright, David's work has appeared in *The New York Times, Best American Essays*, numerous literary and art magazines, and small theater companies. He has written three books about art and architecture.

Taking a New Direction

David Masello

My first day after being fired from an unpleasant job began with a morning visit to the unemployment office, followed by a lunch invitation to New York's fanciest private club. Both events were firsts in my life.

I arrived at the club after a run across town, my suit pockets bulging with Labor Department brochures on "Dressing for Success" and "Your Attitude at Work."

Before we sat for lunch, the hostess led me and three friends into the club's library. Fifth Avenue traffic was a whispering whoosh behind floor-to-ceiling windows. A couple on a settee made a voice-cracking toast, "To France!" When a waiter asked for our drinks order, Katie, a financial manager, replied: "Tomato. Ice. Lemon. Please."—not an unreasonable directive but said with an assurance I found admirable and unsettling.

Soon after we entered the club's ladies' dining room, I the only man, in walked Brooke Astor, the then 99-year-old philanthropist, society figure, and woman-savior of the New York Public Library. Even there at the club, where diners' ancestors have streets and parks named for them, the room quieted and energized with her entrance. People asked their tablemates for cues when it was okay to turn and verify the sighting, take in the contours of her hat.

My friend knew Mrs. Astor and led me to her table. I shook her white-gloved hand, through which I read a network of Braille-like veins.

My friend told Mrs. Astor I was starting a literary magazine.

"Marvelous," Mrs. Astor said in a gritted high Park Avenuese. "We *do* need another journal of letters."

Yes, I planned to staple together a xeroxed sheaf of personal essays and call it *First Person*, but hadn't yet gotten to Kinko's. I held my suit close to my chest as I leaned over to shake her hand goodbye, fearful a list of Labor Department hotlines might fall on her paprika-ed sole.

As one of my lunch companions prepared to return to her job as a *New York Times* reporter, Katie to resume managing the assets of a family for whom streets and parks were named, and my hostess to work on a screenplay about her CIA-directive father, I foresaw an afternoon in my then-fifth-floor walkup hunting down all twelve Combat roach traps I'd secreted years earlier.

As we left the club, Katie and I walked in the same direction, but I sensed she was eager to break free. How odd I probably seemed to her. She must meet many men my age, partners in established firms, handsome, chronometer-watched alphas who dine in their own clubs and hire people to find the roach traps in their second homes. At an intersection, she asked, "Which way?" curling her thumb like a hitchhiker to indicate uptown, downtown. I figured whichever direction I chose, she'd say the opposite.

"Downtown."

"Oh, I'm headed up," she said smoothly.

She offered me her cashmere-gloved paw. She shook with a smart once-up, once-down motion, re-slung her cape and took off, the sidewalk reverberating with her heel-heavy departure.

I retraced the blocks we'd walked. Near Fifth, I saw Brooke Astor leaving the club, struggling to keep open the door against a gust. I held it for her. With one hand, she secured her hat, its wide brim a current of riptide ripples.

"Thank you," she said, "A frightful wind."

She was unable to look me in the eye because the gusts were so furious, ankle-stinging whirlpools of trash spinning on the sidewalk. I was just a kindly stranger. Her driver folded her into the backseat and when the limousine door closed, the small part I played in her day had ended.

The corner I'd been standing on is one of those that is perpetually windy—a result of the position of buildings, Central Park, circumstances unknown. But the moment I turned onto Fifth, it was calm again, a tranquil spring day. I no longer had to close my eyes to the wind. Suddenly, for the first time in my years in Manhattan, with no office to return to, I realized I could go in any direction I wanted.

Kathryn Mayer

Kathryn Mayer is a potty-mouth essayist writing out loud about social issues and midlife angst at www.kathrynmayer.com. She is occasionally funny on Instagram and Threads @kathykatemayer, mostly ignores Facebook and X. She proudly grew four and a half off-the-payroll voting adults, is still in the weeds surviving empty nesting, dictated downsizing, and divorce, and is an unfortunate hospice expert. And yet she still uses cynical optimism to chronicle it all. Her essays appear online, in print, and most often, on fridges sticky with tears, smiles, and swears.

Condom Sense

Kathryn Mayer

There's a Costco-sized box of condoms in our hall closet, opened, right up front, with a handful removed so nobody's counting or keeping track if any go missing. Easy access, no questions asked. I want the teenagers in my life to shoplift them all day long. Or treat 'em like mints, take one. Take two. Just take.

I'd prefer these horny teenagers save it for someone who matters, someone who will love them inside and out, to their very core and soul, and not just until the parents get home.

But it's been proven that such perspective takes time, and often much trial and error, and while that maturation percolates, I want the teens to have all the facts about STIs, pregnancy, responsibility, compassion, accountability—and free and easy access to condoms. Because the only thing safer than a condom is abstinence, and, well, that preacher done gone home for the day.

The condom brigade began when my kid's very gorgeous friend had girls drooling over him: smart, ripped, cuter 'n cute, funny, and every parent in town loved him. Us included. Way too short for my daughter (says she, not me), so since kindergarten, they were buds. Just buds.

Which is how I found out about the Purity Promise Card.

"Your *what*?"

"This," he said, proudly taking his promise card from his wallet and showing me. It was his promise to wait to have sex until marriage. Signed by the priest and himself. Said it right there, "I will wait until marriage," and signed on the dotted line. It was a flimsy piece of regular pink printer paper (why pink?), not even card stock. I knew it wouldn't hold up.

This boy. This young, naive boy whom I've known since kindergarten, who still climbed trees and played manhunt in our yard, was quickly becoming a smokin' hot teenager who, in ninth grade, already had upperclassmen jockeying for prom dibs. And he had only a cheesy sheath of paper to protect him. His brain hadn't caught up to his brawn—yet—but when it did, that card wasn't going to help.

"Listen," I said, "I want to give you something, just in case. I'll be right back." I bounded upstairs without a moment to lose—the weekend was fast approaching!

"Mommm . . ." It started as a low hum and escalated like a fire alarm. "Mom-mom-mommy *don't!*" My daughter's disgust started as a low warning growl, quickly escalating into an emergency broadcast system alerting the boy to the approaching sex-ed tornado coming in. Fast. Take cover!

Which is exactly what I wanted him to do: *take cover.*

"Your promise is perfect, really, it is," I said slowly and deliberately as I came back downstairs, "but do me a favor: Put this in your wallet, would ya buddy? Because with all due respect, on some hot summer night in the back of your parents' minivan, that promise card is gonna get you in a whole lotta trouble, and this might just save your night. And your life. Maybe you'll never need it, but please keep it, just in case. Promises are good, but condoms are a smart back-up plan."

The story got out around town, teasing ensued, then it wasn't long before they started stopping by, just to say hi. Or to pick up a forgotten book. Or cleats. Teenagers. Teammates. Friends. Not-so-much-friends. Boys. Girls. By her senior year, most of my daughter's peers knew where to go when promises made might be broken.

Slowly but surely, the box began emptying. Not all in one weekend, but over the course of high school, clearly somebody was getting something.

Safely, thank you very much.

Edward McCann

Edward McCann, an award-winning writer and producer, is the founder of *Writers Read*, which creates performance opportunities for writers. For over a decade, Ed and a team of dedicated volunteers have worked to present hundreds of stories at dozens of high-quality events with partners like Carnegie Hall, Bryant Park, Vassar College, the National Arts Club, and City Winery. Ed's own writing has appeared in many journals and magazines, including *Country Living, Better Homes & Gardens, Good Housekeeping, The Irish Echo,* and *The Sun*, and he's a regular contributor to *Milieu*, a magazine about design. He and his partner, Richard Kollath, share their Hudson Valley home with a Louisiana rescue mutt named Willie.

The Apology

Edward McCann

I am the son of a man who was quick with his hands and slow to offer any praise; a man who quit drinking years before my birth, but who hadn't quit being angry.

I was twelve and my brother Jim was fourteen in 1975—the last two of six children still at home when my parents sold our house in Queens and moved us to a retirement community in sunny central Florida. I looked at our new home—a pastel, cinder block and stucco house next door to Mom's elderly Aunt Millie and Uncle Harold—with no idea what our future held.

In December, just a few months after we arrived, Uncle Joe's wife, Anne, died in Brooklyn. Millie and Harold needed to get to New York immediately, but a freak snowstorm had closed JFK—or Idlewild, as my father continued to call it long after the name had been changed. Dad offered to drive Millie and Harold the thousand miles home to Brooklyn for their sister-in-law's wake and funeral, so they packed right away and drove through the night.

A week later, my father returned to Florida, to his home surrounded by grapefruit trees and sago palms, no longer looking so angry. The scowl etched into his face from years of furrowed concentration on pipe fittings and technical manuals and crossword puzzles was gone. He sat in his chair at the dining table, sipping an amber drink over ice and telling my mother about the trip, about the great piles of snow, and about watching Uncle Joe photograph his wife's body in the casket.

At twelve I didn't grasp the significance of the alcohol on the table and didn't know it was the first time in decades he'd had anything to drink at all. The remarkable thing was that it was the first time I ever saw my father cry.

Mom busied herself at the sink and Dad set his glass down, dried his eyes with the backs of his balled fists, and beckoned my brother

Jimmy and me toward him. He gathered us in his arms and held us close, something he'd never done before. "I know I haven't always been a good father to you boys," Dad said as fresh tears flowed down his face, "and I'm sorry." His voice broke, and in a strangled sob he added, "I shouldn't have even had you kids; I was too old to be the kind of father you needed."

My older brother and sisters had a father who drank, a man who sometimes sang and played piano or played the spoons against his thigh. That wasn't the man who raised me; I'd gotten a dry drunk with an explosive temper whom I'd never seen touch a piano or a drink. Yet that day, with our arms crossed and tangled around him, Jimmy and I held our father as he wept and trembled; we told him that we loved him, that we wouldn't trade him for any other dad in the world.

The funeral—and then the alcohol Dad sipped—had unlocked something deep inside him, revealing a dimension of the man I'd never seen before. The drink on the table before him was a dose of truth serum, a magic potion; and like the WD-40 in his old tool kit, it had somehow lubricated and loosened a part of him that had long ago rusted and seized.

Even as his health was failing from asbestos exposure and decades of smoking—things that also pre-dated my birth—I noticed that my new, more relaxed and congenial father seemed to tell more jokes, and was enjoying, finally, in his brief retirement, the occasional highball or Tom Collins or beer he'd denied himself for years.

Three years later, at fifteen, I was the last one in the viewing chapel the morning of my father's burial. I placed my palms flat on his chest, cold and unyielding as a block of marble beneath layers of wool and cotton, then rested my warm hands over my father's cold ones. I spoke with him then, telling him things I'd never told anyone and asking questions that can never be answered.

Now decades later, I've moved far away from the pastel world of that Florida retirement community. I don't know what my father would think of the life I'm living today with Richard Kollath in upstate New York, but I feel his presence in a few quiet corners of our house—in the secretary desk where he once sat to write his bills, in his Depression-era, paint-encrusted aluminum stepladder, and in a bucket of his old wrenches I keep in the shed. And I feel him still in the memory of that single apology for the man he wasn't, and the father he wished he'd been.

Malachy McCourt

Malachy McCourt was born in Brooklyn, New York, and from the age of three was raised in Limerick, Ireland. He returned to New York at age twenty, working manual jobs until he became an actor, a career that led to many roles on Broadway, off-Broadway, on television, and in film. Malachy's writing was published in *New York Newsday, National Geographic, Conscience Magazine,* and *The New York Times*. With his brother, Frank, he co-authored the play *A Couple of Blaguards* and he wrote his own *New York Times* bestselling memoir, *A Monk Swimming*. Among his most notable books was *Death Need Not Be Fatal*. Other books included a second memoir, *Singing My Him Song, Danny Boy,* a history of *The Claddagh Ring, Voices of Ireland,* an anthology, and *Malachy McCourt's History of Ireland, Harold Be Thy Name,* and *Bush Lies in State*. Malachy was happily married to Diana for more than four decades, had five grown children, was a grandfather to four, and owed a great deal to his friend Bill W.

My American Dream

Malachy McCourt

Some of us not raised in the U.S. romanticize the life of Americans. We imagine tree-lined avenues with motorcars parked in driveways; we imagine cheery families with beautiful white teeth and warm dispositions living in lovely homes with lawns and flowerbeds, all lit by a friendly sun.

When you grow up abroad you dream of this American life, not imagining that there is poverty here, too, along with disease and disability; you don't think about the laborers, garbage removers, street sweepers, gas station attendants, maids, and gardeners; you don't think about crime and criminals, the jailed and the jailers, or of a populace dreaming of a better life—perhaps elsewhere than America.

I did not dream of going to America to do anything for America, I just thought and dreamt of what it would do for me. I knew I wanted to avoid manual labor and not have to work outdoors. And while I couldn't know just what I would do once I got there, I daydreamed a vision of myself entering a huge office building where I took a lift to ascend to a very high floor. There, a series of desk-bound secretaries would greet me with "Good morning, Mr. McCourt" as I made my way to an office where I'd spend my days making important decisions.

It did not quite turn out that way.

I got a menial job washing dishes, and I did manual labor on the docks. I did some other work loading trucks and bartending before I began acting and appearing on radio and TV shows. As my life in America became more interesting and complicated, I married, fathered two children, and divorced. I remarried, became a father again, ran for governor, wrote books and a play with my brother, Frank, and now have eight grandchildren with a great grandchild on the way. It's been a rich and interesting life, and while I owe much to America, I participated in doing something important for America, too.

My beloved wife, Diana, had a child with a developmental disability from her previous marriage. After our sons Conor and Cormac were born, we had to seek residential care for Nina. And when we ran out of money, we had to move Nina to an institution known as Willowbrook State School.

When we began poking around Willowbrook we discovered large wards filled with people of all ages screaming, blubbering, some completely naked in pools of their own excrement. Some of them sat banging their heads against the wall, causing their blood to flow and mix with the stinking mess on the floor. For fun, some of the attendants had the beleaguered inmates put on sex shows for them. It was a deplorable warehouse of humanity; a notorious place where the most vulnerable human beings were horribly neglected and abused.

Diana and I, along with the relatives of some of the inmates, formed a liaison with radical staff members and a young attorney and television reporter named Geraldo Rivera to expose the innermost savagery of a shocking and inhuman system. Our daughter Nina joined a list of people led by the ACLU and the Legal Aid Society in a lawsuit that took five years and eventually closed down Willowbrook forever, releasing nearly six thousand citizens into relative freedom in their home communities with appropriate support. Nina went on to live a relatively normal life in an apartment with two roommates and twenty-four-hour care, and beyond Willowbrook, there emerged a legal precedent that has changed the lives of people with developmental difficulties in this country forevermore.

At his inauguration, our first Irish-American president said, "Ask not what your country can do for you; ask what you can do for your country." I came to America thinking only about what it could do for me. But helping to change this system for all of America is one of my proudest achievements.

Tracy Doolittle McNally

Tracy Doolittle McNally is the former executive director of Historic Huguenot Street in New Paltz, New York, past president of the Greene County Chamber of Commerce in Catskill, and past vice president of the United Way for Ulster County. Prior to her career in the nonprofit world, Tracy worked in corporate advertising for an international forest products company. Tracy is retired and currently pursuing her lifelong hobbies of genealogy, ballet, and storytelling.

The M Word

Tracy Doolittle McNally

At age thirty-eight, I relocated to live and work in the Hudson Valley. Although jobs were hard to come by, I managed to land one as director of marketing and public relations at Benedictine Hospital, a Catholic hospital in Kingston. This was a big change from my previous corporate world. I knew little about hospital management and less about the Catholic Church, other than that the Church had tried to murder my French Huguenot ancestors in the early 1600s.

Not long after I began working, a Benedictine Sister asked me to assemble a team of four— myself included—to represent the hospital in a trivia contest to benefit another nonprofit agency. I wanted to tell the dear Sister that I'd rather poke needles in my eyes than play trivia, but since I was the new hire, I thought better of it and started searching for other players. I deliberately didn't ask any doctors to participate, because I wanted to have fun and drink with the nurses. Few were game to play, and after multiple strikeouts, a colleague suggested that I approach Dr. Richard McNally. "He knows everything," she said, "music, poetry, Shakespeare, beer making, sports—and he's very nice; not like a doctor at all."

Dr. McNally and I had never met before, but during my first week on the job I'd phoned him for the answer to a serious yet awkward question posed to me by a newspaper reporter during a contentious and controversial hospital merger: "How does a laboratory in a Catholic hospital obtain sperm for fertility testing if the Church prohibits masturbation?" When I relayed the question to the doctor, I avoided using the m word and simply asked, "How do you get sperm?" Dr. McNally replied, "If your mother hasn't told you by now, I'm not sure I can help."

Dr. McNally remembered me when, two months later, I phoned him again, and he consented to join my trivia team. The week before the contest, I'd rented an antique black-sequined dress for an upcoming Halloween party at a haunted Hudson River mansion. Since I couldn't alter the dress's ample bust line, I bought a pair of those silicone breast forms that "increase your bust by two bra cup sizes." The night of the trivia contest, I decided in the parking lot to put the breast forms to the test—to actually wear them and see if they stayed put. Sitting in my car, I scanned the area to make sure no one could see me and slipped them into place. Then off I went with those jelly-like forms wiggling under my red business suit.

Dr. McNally bought me a drink, and the contest began. I contributed little of value to our team, but toward the end of the evening, the God of Trivia threw me a bone with the following question: "Who wrote the poem that begins 'The fog comes on little cat feet?'" No one knew the answer, not even the Good Doctor. But I did. "Carl Sandburg" I said to the judges, ever so pleased with myself for clinching a bottle of wine for the team. I went on to explain to anyone willing to listen how, when I was twelve years old, I wrote an essay about the poem, poking fun at the poet's metaphor in Mr. Kaye's seventh grade English class at Scarsdale Junior High. Twenty-seven years later that essay really paid off.

Ten months later, after that fateful night of trivia, Richard and I were married on Nantucket Island, despite my misleading him with those silicone forms. And in case you're still wondering how the Catholic hospital obtained sperm specimens, it turned out there was a loophole. Although the medical laboratory was located in the hospital, it wasn't actually owned by the hospital per se, enabling the patients to "m" as much as they liked without fear of going blind.

Margarita Meyendorff

Margarita Meyendorff, or Mourka, as she is known, was born displaced in a refugee camp in Germany, far from the opulence of Imperial Russia that was her family's homeland before a series of wars changed everything. She has performed as an actress, dancer, musician, and storyteller at venues throughout the U.S. and Europe, and her memoir, *DP: Displaced Person*, has been translated into Russian. She's also recently published *Flipping the Bird*, a series of short stories based on her remarkable journeys. She's now at work on her third book, entitled *The Magic Bus*, that will chronicle the adventures she and her husband had in their 1991 Volkswagen pop-up Westfalia camper.

Chewing Gum

Margarita Meyendorff

I am six years old and obsessed with chewing gum. Gum is a forbidden substance. My parents don't allow me to chew it. Maybe chewing gum is not an aristocratic thing to do and we are aristocrats. Maybe it's an American custom and we are Russian, and Russians don't chew gum. I don't know. All I know is that I am a Russian aristocrat and for this little baroness, chewing gum is as desirable as it is forbidden.

I start out by stealing gum from the grocery store on the corner of Main Street and Franklin in Nyack where my parents do their weekly shopping. I love Bazooka the best. It's big in the mouth and I love the pink color, the sugary texture, and the colorful comics that go with the label. Of course, I can't read the comics as I don't read English yet, but I love the pictures. I steal the gum, bring it home, hide it under my pillow in my bed, and chew it after my father and I recite the Russian Orthodox night prayer in church Slavonic: "Heavenly King, Comforter, Spirit of Truth, Who art everywhere and fulfilling all the treasure of good and Giver of life. Come and abide in me and cleanse me from all evil . . . Save me."

Sometimes I fall asleep chewing gum and find the wad next to me in the morning—a big pink cold lump of goo. I promptly put the wad back in my mouth, chew it a little, drain all the sugar out, climb out of bed, and finally spit it into the toilet and flush. All traces gone.

Inevitably I am caught stealing the gum. We are in the store, and I swipe the gum and hold it in my pockets—one pack in each pocket. My hands in my pockets for so long rouses my parents' suspicions, and finally they ask me to take my hands out of my pockets and show them everything I have. I am so ashamed. My parents escort me to the checkout lady. With the Bazooka in my hand and in broken English I have to confess to the cashier that I have taken the gum without paying for it. Nothing like this has ever happened. I have shamed my parents, all Russians, disgraced the aristocracy. I have blasphemed the Eastern Orthodox God who will now refuse to save me. I apologize and tell everyone standing around in my heavily accented English—"I vill never steal gum again." And I don't.

I graduate from stealing gum to scraping up old gum from the sidewalk, putting it in my mouth, and chewing it. I enjoy the vestiges of minty-ness and the sweetness that remain in it. Some of the pieces have a little gravel or dust stuck to them. No matter; it is gum and I love it. Chewing sidewalk gum goes on for a while, until finally, I get an abscess on my lip. The abscess is like a large pimple that grows and grows. No one has a clue where this pimple has come from, but I have my suspicions—my punishment has begun.

In the future, whenever I am offered gum, even when someone tempts me with a demonstration of a snap and a crackle and a surreal expanding big bright bubble of neon pink Bazooka, my answer is a vehement "No thanks!" Russian aristocracy notwithstanding, I have chewed my last.

Brad Mislow

Brad Mislow is a New York–based writer whose work has been seen as an original on-camera commentary on CBS News *Sunday Morning*, humor pieces in the *Jewish Review of Books*, and within the copy of so many TV commercials that try to convince consumers to buy things they don't really need. Since losing his full-time job, he's grown a following on LinkedIn with #stayingpositivewithbrad, which offers readers an unconventional point of view on being unemployed. He lives in the Bronx with his two adult-ish children and Rosie, a misunderstood pit bull mix. He will not be taking questions at this time.

Baby Got Back . . . Hair

Brad Mislow

I have back hair. A lot. From my neck on down. My father had it. So did my grandfathers, uncles, and male cousins. Back hair is a strong genetic trait among Ashkenazi Jewish men. Look, Eastern Europe is cold. And who knows how many times my ancestors had to flee in the dead of winter from hordes of anti-Semites during pogrom season. Evolution decided that warmth meant survival. Thus, hair sprouted on our backs, and I am here to tell the tale.

Since I grew up around so much body hair, I never thought anything of it. My father was a bald, well-built man, with a tremendous amount of blond body hair. He was never self-conscious and had no shame going shirtless. As my back gradually got hairier in my twenties, I never considered grooming. However, I did opt to swim with a T-shirt. One time at Jones Beach, a very hairy man walked past me, and some nearby drunk twenty-somethings started making Wookiee noises. My shirt stayed on.

Let's face it: Back hair has no sex appeal. You don't see Hollywood A-listers flashing their hairy backs on screen. Hairy men in movies are mocked, or made to seem ape-like, and they never end up getting the girl. I mean, every time they remake King Kong, he dies.

So one very hot summer day I made an appointment to get a haircut at a neighborhood salon with a woman named Annie. She was Albanian American and grew up in the Bronx. She was around my age and kind of cute. She regularly shaved the hair on the back of my neck as part of her service. On this hot summer day, she pulled my shirt collar and peeked down.

"Hmm," she said. "Come with me to the back room. Let's make you feel better."

This was all starting to sound like the opening lines of countless porn movies, but I was married at the time, and there were other customers around, so yeah. I followed her into a darkly lit back room where there was a massage table and other spa accessories. Total change of vibe.

"Take off your shirt," she said.

Okay, now I'm starting to wonder where this is headed. I'm staring face to face with Annie, shirtless. I'm shirtless. She's dressed.

"Turn around," she said.

I hear the click and the hum of her shears, which begin to glide down my back. I'm getting shorn like a sheep. Annie said she did this for her brothers growing up, and it was not a big deal.

"You're going to feel so much cooler."

She continued until my back was smooth and hairless. I looked in the mirror and saw freckles I haven't seen in decades. She rubbed in some cooling lotion and instructed me to put my shirt back on. It was weird. I could actually feel my shirt on my back. I looked on the floor and there was a pile of all the shorn hair. She swept and it filled an entire dustpan. She held up her shears.

"Do you have one of these at home? I recommend one."

I learned later that this was a one-time deal. All further shearings would have to be done on my own, which involves a lot of bodily contortions and thorough sweeping. Was it worth it? I decided in the long run, it wasn't. It's not like I'm a male model or a lifeguard or some other profession that involves long periods of shirtlessness. So why bother? Who was I trying to impress? But here's how I really made peace with it. In the dating pool, especially among middle-aged women who prefer Jewish men, back hair is a nonissue. In fact, they like it. Or they just liked me and decided it's just part of the whole package. And that makes sense, because like most gifts, I come fully wrapped.

Annabel Monaghan

Annabel Monaghan is the national bestselling author of *Summer Romance, Same Time Next Summer,* and *Nora Goes Off Script,* published by G.P. Putnam's Sons. She says writing these love stories has probably been the most fun she's ever had. Pre-Nora, she wrote fiction for young adults and a column for not-so-young adults. She grew up in Los Angeles, and nearly every one of her relatives still lives in Southern California. She attended Duke University where she studied English, earned an MBA from The Wharton School of the University of Pennsylvania, and has a brief history as an investment banker. She also used to teach novel writing at the Writing Institute at Sarah Lawrence College. She lives in the suburbs of New York City with her family, including a little dog who sheds.

The Game of Life

Annabel Monaghan

The great thing about Candy Land and Chutes and Ladders is that they can be played in less than fifteen minutes and take very little mental effort. Even so, when my husband comes home from work, I can still add "played a board game with the kids" to my list of heroic accomplishments. I could be on the phone (or even writing this article) and breeze through one of those games, no problem. Unfortunately, my five-year-old has developed an unhealthy interest in The Game of Life, the only game I own that is possibly more complicated than life itself.

At first I try to convince him that the little cars that lead us down Life's path are there to be zoomed, and that whoever gets to the end first wins. But he isn't having it. So I figure if we are going to have to play, we'll do it right. I'll teach him a few Life lessons and get the dialogue going about the world around us. You know, actual parenting, like on TV. We are just finishing up the ten minutes it takes to set the game up when I remember that he doesn't know how to read. I reinvent the game to read the events of his life to him as they unfold.

The game starts at age eighteen, and I am pleased to see that he chooses to go to college. Having made such a wise choice, he is faced with many career options after graduation. I encourage him to choose the accounting job because it comes with the possibility of the highest salary card. To my horror, he chooses to be a singer because, he claims, that's what he likes to do. Why would he spend his life doing something he doesn't like just for the money? Sigh. He's got a lot to learn.

Meandering through Life, we each stop to get married. He thinks carefully before choosing a pink peg for his spouse rather than a blue one. He buys a house, which he chooses for its color. Later, I have to inform him that his house was robbed and that he should have bought the insurance as I told him to. I didn't know I'd get robbed. Ah, an actual Life lesson! He rejoices every time he lands on a square that gives him another baby. He fills up his car with the allotted four children and then hoards the extras, laying them at the feet of his other kids in the back seat. (I have another son who likes to collect the child pegs too but leaves them on the side of the board with his money, claiming, "I don't want those kids riding in my car." I like to refer to him as The Smart One.)

Life gets more complicated as you move along. He wants to know what a Pulitzer Prize is and if it comes with candy. He wants to know who has the Solution to Pollution and why anyone would want to swim across the English Channel. I can only answer one of those. At some point I find myself explaining what a stock is, then what a dividend is, and what taxes are for. And how dividends are taxed at a lower rate than ordinary income and why Warren Buffet doesn't really like that.

As Life winds down, we are laden with cash and real estate and lucky heirs, and we race toward retirement. Now retirement is a tricky thing; if you can afford it you get to go to Millionaire Estates and if you can't you're relegated to Countryside Acres. Before you enter either, you sell your house, the price of which is determined by a random spin of the wheel. That actually sounds about right.

Life ends, and I realize I've just spent a full hour explaining to a five-year-old how life works. I wait for the applause and maybe a little confetti as we each count up our money to determine who wins. And because I chose the rejected accounting job with the coveted yellow salary card, I have the most money. I tell him with great humility that I have won, and he has lost. He shakes his head and tells me, "I have the most family. I win."

I may need to rethink a few things.

Anthony C. Murphy

Anthony C. Murphy grew up in Lancashire, England. He has worked as a postman, toured Europe as a roadie, and been an associate producer of live poetry nights and open mic events. He's performed at spoken word events in the UK and here in the U.S. for fifteen years, including several *Writers Read* shows. A member of Irish American Writers and Artists, he's a regular contributor at their salons in Manhattan and elsewhere. Anthony has three kids and two dogs who, he says, are all lovely, in their own way. At home in northern Westchester, Anthony brews nourishing ales, enjoys walking the dogs and watching the birds, and volunteers at his daughter's school, where he shares his love of nonsense poetry with the kids. He's published a novel, *Shiftless*, and several poetry chapbooks.

Another Family Plot

Anthony C. Murphy

"So?" the barmaid asks.

"A pint of that." I point and dig coins from my pockets.

"What's up?"

"I lost my dad." I sigh.

"Uh huh!" She's listening. "Have you phoned anyone?"

"It's not like that. He was in an urn," I say. "My bag was stolen. I was at a party."

"Well. Okay . . . Where did you last see him?" she asks, matter-of-factly.

"Dublin," I say. And she laughs. She snorts a big one and curses and crosses herself to keep the demons at bay. "Holy Feckin' Jeezus! Do you even know where ye are?"

"No," I say.

"Well, I hope you said your goodbyes!" she says and tuts at me.

"Yeah," I say. "Not really. I just brought the ashes from England to get buried back home in Cork."

"Here," she says, handing me a pint. "You're in Wicklow!" She shakes her head.

"Thanks!" I do remember the train, vaguely.

The stout burns my throat, but I don't care. I wonder if this has happened before. The stealing of an urn! It must have happened before. Maybe they thought there was something valuable in it?

I sit there sipping and feeling sorry for myself. A few more patrons enter the pub and are familiar with me. Sharon lights a fag and blows the smoke out of the side of her mouth and picks a piece of tobacco out of her teeth—I guess it could be something else. "So, what are you going to do?"

"Can I get one of those?" I ask, pointing to her cigarette.

"No." She considers. "You have to earn it."

I am feeling hungry now with my emptied belly. I look about the bar, but they don't have much. "Can I have a pickled egg please?"

"Sure," says Sharon. "It's your funeral . . . Sorry!"

"I like them," I say. I tuck into it; it's like a chemistry lesson exploding in my mouth, but it helps with my reality, it gives me a jolt. "Will you let me collect glasses for you tonight?" I ask, cheeks full of acidic protein. "Then I can earn it."

Sharon thinks. "Why not?" She puffs. "But I tell you, it's quiet on Mondays." She gives me one of her cigarettes. I agree with her, but I have a lot going on. I have to get to Cork for the funeral service. And I have no remains to bury. Where are you, Dad? My head is clear as a hangover. I check my socks for cash.

"Sharon, can I have the whole jar of eggs please? And another pint."

"Where are you going with this?" she asks, but she gives me the jar. The weight and size of it are comparable to the urn. Of course it's glass and not plastic. I'll have to explain something to my Aunt Maureen, but not that I haven't got my dad with me . . . And there are only ten eggs left. "It's doable!" I say to Sharon.

"Sure. Weirdo!" she says.

"Okay, everyone, the pickled eggs are on me! Do it for the old feller!" I shout and raise the jar aloft with both hands like I've just won the cup. I hear one whoop and I have a few takers but . . . I have to eat most of the eggs myself. It's a chastening experience. I know I can throw them away but that's such a waste! I probably won't eat for a while anyway. My stomach revolts a little, but I manage.

All night I collect empties for my new friends and clean out the ashtrays; I stash all of their fag ash in the old pickle jar. Later, I have to sift it a little, but at least I have a new dad, although he's lost weight. He smells of vinegar and old smoke, but he would anyway.

I tighten the lid on him.

Ellen Nenner

Music has always been a grand passion for **Ellen Nenner**. It propelled her from New York's famous High School of Music and Art to the even more famous Juilliard School. Today she is a trustee at MasterVoices, a not-for-profit performing-arts institution dedicated to the power of the human voice. In addition, Ellen studied economics and philosophy at Mt. Holyoke, studied urban planning at the New School, and was a writer and editor for McKinsey. Luckily for us, Ellen also studied at the Writing Institute at Sarah Lawrence College, where her facility with words took her in new directions. These days she is working on a book of connected essays and short stories for her daughters, Lisa and Jackie, and her grandson, Kolby.

The Greener

Ellen Nenner

I am in my garden in Truro, a small town wedged between Wellfleet and Provincetown on the outer cape. September has brought its usual cool weather. I have started to convert the house from the focus of dinner parties and family visits. From a vacation option for widowed friends not yet comfortable or smart enough to reach out to live what's left of life to a state of suspension: all systems off, bird feeders collected, washed, and put in the lower basement. The house will now sleep until early next May.

I spend some time pruning and tidying what is left of my heirloom tomato plants. There is nothing healthy or alive now, no fruit, only wasted bodies with thin, scrawny arms and stems so weak and dehydrated that they no longer have the strength to remain upright. So why am I bent over, snipping here and there, making things neat, sprucing up plants whose lives are spent?

I am thinking of another day, another time. I am at home in New York, standing in Ray's clothes closet, deciding how I should dress his body. He is in the funeral home, awaiting my decision. The casket will be closed. Our daughters, Jackie and Lisa, have already said their final goodbyes at the hospital. Who would see him? Who would notice what he wore? But I want him to look every bit the Polish Prince, a name my college friends dubbed him when we began to date seriously.

I pace back and forth in the closet, sliding the heavy walnut suit hangers he preferred back and forth, stopping in front of this jacket or that suit. I remember the pains Manny, the head tailor at Paul Stuart, took to ensure that the fit of his jackets was perfect. He knew just how much padding would equalize the one-inch difference between Ray's right and left shoulders; the cost of carrying his heavy medical bag on eight to ten house calls a day. I finally select a navy blazer with beautiful gold buttons, a blue and white striped shirt, and a crimson, blue, and white paisley tie. I always had the last word about the shirts and ties.

Ray was a Polish immigrant and a Holocaust survivor. After he was liberated from a Nazi concentration camp, he was sent to a displaced persons' camp outside of Munich. He attended Ludwig Maximilian University's medical school in Munich, graduated in 1950, and immigrated to the United States.

When he came to New York he spoke very little English and understood even less. Two or three movies a day taught him enough to pass the exams he needed to continue his medical studies. But the English language continued to trip him up for the forty years we were married.

"Sometimes the words just don't make sense. I remember Mort Green and his wife inviting me to dinner at a fancy restaurant," he said, smiling at the memory. "Mort had more house calls a day than any other general practitioner in Queens, and he let me cover for him on the weekends. I needed the money, and I needed that dinner too.

"I suppose I was what people called a greener—meaning an unrefined, newly arrived immigrant. A lot of the food on the menu was unfamiliar to me until I spotted halibut steak. I absolutely knew what steak was."

He laughed, remembering how he forced himself to eat the fish—a food he avoided throughout our marriage.

So why am I bent over, snipping here and there, making things neat, sprucing up plants whose lives are spent?

Because words sometimes just don't make sense.

Jack O'Connell

Native New Yorker **Jack O'Connell** lives these days on Long Island with his wife, Margaret. He knows how lucky he is to be not only an actor by profession and choice, but also a "working actor" with dozens of credits. You may recognize him from his roles in film and TV, among them *Doubt, Big Night, Inside Llewyn Davis, Mad Men, Nurse Jackie, Vinyl,* and *The Marvelous Mrs. Maisel.* He recently had a guest starring role in the new Netflix hit *Kaleidoscope* and is making the festival rounds in *La Locura*, a series dealing with Alzheimer's.

Almost on the Waterfront

Jack O'Connell

In May of 1991, as an aspiring actor, I was invited to participate in a stage reading of the classic *On the Waterfront* as part of the Westhampton Beach Writers Festival.

The cast, including some professional actors, would read the play in celebration of the fortieth anniversary of the film. Budd Schulberg, a local resident who had partnered with Stan Silverman to write the play, would oversee this staged reading.

My role was longshoreman Runty Nolan (KO Duggan in the film), who gets murdered in the first act when a sling loaded with cargo gets dropped on him for standing up to the bosses. The reading went so well, we were asked for an encore at the John Drew Theatre in East Hampton that August. As several cast members would not be available due to summer commitments and had to be replaced, the director, Kelly Patton, called and said that Mr. Schulberg would like me to read the priest, Father Barry. Thrilled even though it was still a staged reading, I worked on the lines as if it were a full-scale production.

We received wonderful reviews in *The East Hampton Star*, and by the following summer we were taking the show on the road. First to Putney, Vermont, where we would give two readings at Landmark College. Our cast and crew were fed and housed by local sponsors. My son Henry and I stayed in a furnished treehouse on the Dodge family estate.

In spring 1993 we headed to Hoboken, New Jersey, where the film was shot. With new faces in the cast, we set the stage in a former industrial space, a perfect backdrop. A younger actor was brought in to relieve me of my priestly duties, so I took over the role of Johnny Friendly, union boss.

Rumors were circulating that this would be a backers' audition with a possible move to a showcase production in Manhattan. And after our first performance in Hoboken, a tall, handsome woman approached me, introducing herself as Patricia Kennedy Lawford, a long-time friend of Mr. Schulberg. The "big shots" were watching.

A few months later, November 1993, we opened for a twelve-performance showcase production with original music by Leonard Bernstein and mood-setting lighting at Theatre Row, West Forty-Second Street. Opening night was thrilling. Elia Kazan, who had directed the film, was in the audience, as was Jerry Orbach, Chris Noth, and many other actors, agents, and casting people.

The show was a huge hit. After the final performance, the champagne flowed at the cast party along with hors d'oeuvres from Zabar's. Just as exciting, a legitimate agent asked me to drop by his office to discuss representation.

Then in early 1994 the word came down: *On the Waterfront* was moving to Broadway. The show would be produced by Dodger Productions with a planned May 1995 opening four years after our first reading in Westhampton Beach. What a ride it had been!

Except for the fact that my ride was over. Not one of the showcase actors would be in the Broadway cast. I was distraught.

About one week before previews began, I walked over to the Brooks Atkinson Theatre to see who would be playing my character. It was like seeing an old girlfriend all dressed up in heels walking away with her new beau.

I'm not sure if I felt vindicated, but the Broadway transfer closed after eight performances. And six years later, while I was playing the lead in a production of Arthur Miller's *All My Sons*, Budd Schulberg appeared in my dressing room after a matinee performance. He said with his stammer that he had nothing to do with the casting for the Broadway version of his show. I stepped back a foot, looked at him, and said in a British accent, "What show was that, lovey?"

He laughed, I laughed, and we hugged.

I guess that's Show Biz.

Irene O'Garden

Irene O'Garden has won or been nominated for prizes in nearly every writing category from stage to e-screen, hardcovers, literary magazines, and anthologies. Irene's critically acclaimed play *Women on Fire* played to sold-out houses off-Broadway. Her play *Little Heart*, about artist Corita Kent, premiered at Jewel Theatre in Santa Cruz in 2023, which led to the new play commission she recently completed, *Alice in Widowland*. Irene has published several books, including two memoirs, *Fat Girl and Risking the Rapids*; a book of essays, *Glad to Be Human*; and *Fulcrum*, her first poetry collection.

An Argument with Water

Irene O'Garden

Journey's end, our final blue Aegean day. Shockingly, you book a swim trip. You hate swimming. A pool's for cooling ankles, a shiver dip on triple-digit days. You carry from another life an argument with water, an argument unsettled by your swimming-teacher father.

Did you forget it? Let it go? Or did you test it, that brilliant sea-smashed morning boarding the tidy charter?

A dozen tawny bodies unfolding on the deck. Young entwining hands, unlike ours, ringless. A friendly bunch. Gentle laughter, quiet marvels. Swelling sails, whitecaps, gem-blue waves. Soon, an oxblood promontory. Smiles. Yours, too. Fricative shutter clicks.

Fathoms evaporate. Red rock yields to chalk-white stone. We anchor. I have arguments, but none with water. Off the stern I slip. Under glacier-y crumbling towers, I frolic in the cove; you snap shots from the deck. On we sail. Lime rock yields to runneled pumice, pitch-black beach. Another anchoring.

Is the answer in the fine professor's lecture months ago: "Swim, swim the hot springs if you can?" What made you leap your ancient lapping fear, slide into this second bay, tread water next to me, whisper as we clamber up, "I'll stay in longer, next time?" Next time, why did doubt leap with you?

Third anchor drop.

We ladder to the water, push off, aiming for the golden cove: balmy hot springs maybe twenty boat-lengths off—aiming to relax, but suddenly swells churned by swimmer-loaded boats—everyone's longing to float, to relax—saltwater spasms toss us, lurch us, keeping our heads above water now a living idiom. I swim on, glance for you over my bobbing shoulder.

"I'm not doing so well," you gasp.

I plunge to you, hold you. *It's fine. We'll swim to that rock*—miraculous skinny upright poking up just where we need it, miraculous chain looped over it—*Grab this, I'll swim back for life jackets. Breathe. We'll be fine.*

Did I doubt for a moment your strength, your survival? Never. You'd never die now, on the brink of such wonder. But I felt your doubt and your fear, for you swim and surf in emotion, fearlessly challenge its swells.

Hold on, I'll be back with a lifejacket.

I don't want to leave you alone with your fear.

Instead, we conjure up—miraculous—a young man brisking through the surges. "Can I bring you some life jackets?" "Yes!" Later, on deck, we note on his shoulders: scars, peculiar as wing stubs.

We talk about it, as we always talk. You insist you called to me for help. "Not aloud," I said. "But that's why I glanced when I did." After years of listening, silent and aloud are one.

You like to say I saved your life. I maintain no life is saved against its will, and if I heard you call me inwardly, I also heard you tell me not to worry.

After all, you had breath to speak.

Why did you book a swim trip? You can say it was for me, or hot springs, but you dove into your argument with water, headlong into courage, fear, and rescue. Through emotion you are not afraid to swim. Where your broken father had his argument.

Where full fathom five, he lies.

Anna Geraldine Paret

Anna Geraldine Paret first came to America over thirty years ago as an investment banker transferred from London. Subsequently, she has been a docent at Jasper Ridge Biological Preserve at Stanford University and a naturalist at Sheldrake Environmental Center in Larchmont, New York. She is a Scott Meyer Award short-story finalist whose work has been published in *Orbis, Inscape,* and *Ghost Town Literary Magazine*. She and her husband currently divide their time between New York City and London, where their children live and work.

The Greenest Shade of Green

Anna Geraldine Paret

The brunette realtor in ballet flats pointed out, with a barely perceptible straightening of her shoulders, that the majority of Larchmont homeowners are very well educated and (therefore) that the schools here are marvelous. Certainly in the Great Outdoors beyond my front door, in my neighborhood known locally as The Woods, it seems that every other housewife has a master's degree; every third, a PhD.

Rachel (MS) ran a Fortune 500 company before she ran the PTA. The mower-and-blower who tends her garden was the first member of his family to graduate middle school. Rachel instructs him, with a bestowing sweep of her arm, to program her sprinkler system. Perhaps she can figure out how to telephone him when it's raining so that he can come and switch it off.

To be fair, Rachel's yard is perfect, her grass the greenest shade of green. I heard—I suspect I was supposed to hear—her telling Mr. Travis Next Door how to get rid of crabgrass and clover. It is unfortunate that Rachel has such a perfect view of my garden from her house.

Mr. Travis Next Door has a couple of sons in high school. We hear them. Sometimes they're loud and late, but they're in high school. Rachel said to me, "Those boys are out of control. And Mr. Travis is too much of a pushover. He should say something to them."

I thought, *Didn't you ever do anything stupid in high school, you self-righteous cow? I bet you did because everyone does, not only Mr. Travis Next Door's kids.*

Rachel continued, "Mr. Travis should stop being a friend to those boys and start being their role model."

I said, quietly, "We're not there yet, Rachel." Rachel and I both have kids in middle school. In middle school, with the mower-and-blower's son.

Rachel has a cat. Mr. Travis Next Door has a dog. I heard—I'm pretty sure I was supposed to hear—Rachel telling Mr. Travis Next Door that he should make sure that his dog doesn't bark before 10 a.m. because her twelve-year-old really needs to sleep in on a Saturday. ("We're thinking about *Harvard*.")

Mr. Travis Next Door said, "Please keep your cat indoors. It's killing the birds in my yard."

I thought, "Way to go, Mr. Travis Next Door."

Next: Rachel's son (the Harvard prospect in sixth grade with the long, greasy bangs) took up the electric guitar. I heard Mr. Travis Next Door say to Rachel, "Please ask your son not to play the guitar after nine p.m. My dog really needs his sleep."

So when I walk my dog in the rain (a dog's got to do what a dog's got to do) and Rachel's sprinklers go off, catching me below the umbrella, and I feel a rumble of irritation like the tiny bubbles that skim across the bottom of a pan of water before it erupts in a boil, I offer up a silent prayer to Mr. Travis Next Door, then lob a loaded poo bag onto the greenest grass in The Woods.

Cari Pattison

Cari Pattison, a native of Kansas City, serves as Co-Pastor of Rye Presbyterian Church in Rye, New York. Prior to that she pastored congregations elsewhere in the Catskills and Westchester County. Over five years, she backpacked 1,800 miles of the Appalachian Trail and adopted a hardy little hiker dog named Ollie. When not in the woods or teaching yoga, Cari's at work on a memoir about her Appalachian Trail thru-hike: the feats, fractures, and unlikely friendships. Cari has been published in *The Huffington Post, TheTrek.co,* and *d365.org* and has been featured on podcasts for *WritersRead* and *Mighty Blue on the Appalachian Trail.* She adores her three nieces and nephew, and gets back to the Midwest often to visit them.

A Fling and a Prayer

Cari Pattison

Johnny's Match.com profile showed him in red pajamas, seated on a front-porch step with two Scotty dogs. A picture someone's mom would take on Christmas. His face seemed to say, "Happy Holidays. I'll be your first date."

The week before, my church friend and I had met for lunch. With four children, a husband, and two beautiful homes, she surprised me by saying, "I kind of envy you, you know." I laughed. "Why?" She smiled. "You're going to have first kisses again."

That's optimistic, I thought as I got into my car, the divorce papers still fresh on the passenger seat.

The night of the date, I walked briskly through Bryant Park in my red wool coat and umbrella, bracing against the rain. In my pocket I felt the scrap of paper I'd scribbled a prayer on in the train: "Just let us both have fun."

I straightened my dress and adjusted my leather boots. My stomach tightened as I sidestepped puddles toward the restaurant. I could hear my BodyFit teacher's voice saying: "Shoulders back, chin up, abs in, smile."

True to his pictures plus a few pounds, Johnny was brown haired, round of face, and right around my age. He had a Brooklyn accent, a Polish last name, and a stature just taller than mine. Wearing a brown houndstooth jacket and a toothy mischievous grin, he took my coat and ushered me to our corner booth. Smacking his strawberry gum, he said, "You made it."

He ordered wine and I nervously took out my hair band. He reached over and smoothed his finger across my forehead. "No, keep it up," he said. "I like it."

Over salad he told me about his days of skipping school, selling drugs, and getting arrested. He scooted closer, stroking his hand on my thigh. "I'm not used to going out with good girls," he said. I tilted my head, "What makes you think I'm good?" I'd said nothing about what I do for a living. He paused. "You don't swear, you're polite, and you're dressed"— his eyes moved down my chest, past my waist, and back up—"conservative."

I looked down at my form-fitted black shift. The fabric was even shiny. It was like in sixth grade, when I showed up at Scott's bar mitzvah wearing my best Sunday-school dress—a white frock with three pastel bows—while the other girls slid by in strapless sequined gowns. Sexy was always a few steps ahead of me. Our sauteed scallops arrived, rimmed with caramel-brown glaze, and I cut mine slowly. "This is fun," I said to myself. "We're having fun." After months of court dates, tax forms, and moving boxes, "fun" was an alien concept. An island vacation you earned a trip to.

Johnny ordered us more wine and leaned closer, his face inches from mine. His eyes in the dim light were unusually round and open—so much white around the iris. Like the eyes of the possum or raccoon that beamed at me when I took out the garbage at night, I couldn't decide if I found them playful or frightening.

He squeezed my hand and whispered, "Let's kiss now and get the tension over with." Before I could formulate an answer, his mouth pressed to mine and our heads weaved together with overlapping lips, negotiating noses, and fluttering eyelids. The sheer proximity of a man's voice and face and skin startled me.

The only other man I'd ever kissed was my ex-husband, our first time on a concrete ledge outside a grad-student swing dance. I had closed my eyes and waited for something to happen. I didn't know you had to move your mouth. I didn't know you didn't have to marry the first man you kissed. I tried not to think about this as Johnny moved his mouth from my lips to my cheek to the top of my ear.

We walked to Grand Central to catch my train and he swiftly pulled me to the wall around the corner from the Forty-Second Street entrance. It felt like someone had flipped the switch of every one of my cells to "on." "Why leave now?" Johnny murmured, his breath warm near my neck.

I felt the crumpled-up prayer in my pocket.

"Tomorrow's Sunday," I said.

"So? Sunday?" he shrugged. "Sleep in, football . . ."

I thought about the ankle-length black wool robe I'd be wearing early the next day, the table of bread and wine I'd stand behind. I tried to picture Johnny there. "I should probably tell you," I said. "I'm a minister."

John Pielmeier

John Pielmeier began his career with the internationally-acclaimed play and movie *Agnes of God.* Since then he's had three more plays mounted on Broadway and over twenty-five film, television movies and miniseries produced. Scribner published his first novel, *Hook's Tale*, to wonderful reviews and his theatrical adaptation of it premiered in Houston in October 2021. His adaptation of William Peter Blatty's *The Exorcist* toured the U.K. after its acclaimed West End run, and is on its way to New York. He's received the Humanitas Award (plus two nominations), five Writers' Guild Award nominations, a Gemini nomination, an Edgar Award, Camie Award, Christopher Award, and his projects have won a Gemini Award and been nominated for the Emmy Award and the Golden Globe.

Girlfriends

John Pielmeier

Their names were Mart and Alison, and they came to visit us on occasion when I was a boy, and once or twice we went to visit them. They were school teachers and lived together on the top floor of an old brick house. Mart was tall and thin and wore her dark hair in a bun; Alison was shorter and red haired and was the kind of woman once called "handsome." Her full name was Alison Douglas, which translated in my five-year-old mind as "Alice and Douglas," but my mother referred to them as "Mart and Alison"—which sounded to me like Martin Alison. It was all so confusing, but oddly appropriate, their names linked as though they were one person, half female, half male, which strikes me even today as not incorrect.

Most of my mother's girlfriends were of the same physical mold. They were either thin and wiry or square and muscular, and all of them were unmarried but for one who had several children and a mustache. Most were gym teachers, and my mother would describe them as "outdoorsy." They first met when she worked as a secretary for the Girl Scouts; they were leaders and administrators, and they were all very fond of her. Whenever they visited, she welcomed them with a kindness shadowed by a certain reluctance I never completely understood. I liked them; they were fun to be around, and they were comfortable in their bodies in ways that other women weren't. They were independent, and they seemed happy.

My mother and her girlfriends spent the summers of the 1930s at a Girl Scout camp near their hometown. All were camp counselors, and they bonded, I imagine, sitting around a campfire late at night after their young charges were in bed, talking of the girls and their teenage problems, and celebrating their own love of being in the great outdoors away from civilization and the tyranny of men.

My mother's boss, a woman named Billie, introduced my mother to my father, and my mother always spoke of Billie with great affection, still remembering the sorrow she suffered when Billie moved to another city and another Girl Scout office. She and Billie exchanged Christmas cards every year, and when I was grown I arranged for my mother and Billie to reconnect. I met Billie for the first time then: She was square and muscular and very outdoorsy. My mother was happy to see her, but the meeting was a little awkward: They didn't have a lot to say to each other and they never saw each other again.

Our next-door neighbor Georgetta once referred to one of my mother's girlfriends as a lesbian. Mother was incensed. It was as if Georgetta had accused the woman, in the paranoia of the 1950s, of being a Russian spy. Of course, in the spirit of that metaphor, all of my mother's girlfriends spoke with thick Russian accents; still, my mother refused to recognize their foreign allegiance. Her Catholicism, and the tenor of the times, denied these women approval. But when her closest friend—a solid woman named Marian who had a contagious laugh and eyes that squinted with warmth—moved in with another woman, my mother refused to judge her. She prayed for her, I'm certain, but she always welcomed Marian gladly when her friend came to visit.

The happiest six months of my mother's life was when she served as a substitute girls' gym teacher at my high school. The girls confided in her, and they loved her. Years later, when my wife and I celebrated our tenth anniversary with a party and a dance, my mother spent the evening cutting a rug with a female friend of ours. "Your mother's a terrific dancer," our friend told us later. "She would have made a great lesbian."

Jennifer Rawlings

Jennifer Rawlings is an award-winning writer and performer whom you may have seen on stations as divergent as Comedy Central, PBS, and FOX. Or you might have caught one of her TEDx talks. Jennifer has also performed in over 350 military shows in various locations, including Iraq and Afghanistan. Her critically acclaimed directorial debut, *Forgotten Voices: Women in Bosnia*, screened at film festivals worldwide. In 2014 Jennifer was named one of the "21 Change Makers of the 21st Century" by *Women's E News*. She's currently touring her solo show, *I Only Smoke in War Zones*.

A Kansas Tan

Jennifer Rawlings

Salina, Kansas. I was sixteen years old. Dusk was settling in just as my dad and I settled on the front porch. My dad in his lawn chair—Pabst Blue Ribbon, pipe full of tobacco—me on the porch swing with a pink can of TAB.

The mosquitoes were chewing my Coppertoned legs, but I didn't care, I had an agenda:

"Dad, can I have some money to buy tickets for the Summer Jam concert?"

This was going to be the most important concert of my life. Reo Speedwagon, Styx, John Cougar . . . before the Mellancamp. EVERYONE was going; I had to be there too.

Puff, puff, on the pipe . . . tamp down with the corner of a matchbook. My dad's answer, slow as a smoke ring: "It's time you earn your own spending money—get a job for the summer."

"DAD! I don't have time for a job. I have THINGS to do. Why do you hate me?" I sobbed. I ran up the stairs to my bedroom, dropped the needle on Supertramp's *Breakfast in America.*

I wasn't lazy; I didn't have time to work.

I had my driver's license, though. I needed to drive with my friends to the mall . . . to the liquor store. We loved the liquor store on State Street. It was called State Street Liquor. The owner had the posture of a question mark and despite his horn-rimmed glasses, he wasn't that sharp. He carded me every time because the sign said, "We card everyone." And every time this sixteen-year-old walked out with some hooch.

We drove to the banks of the Smokey Hill River, drank beer, and inhaled the smokes we had swiped from our older siblings.

I had a boyfriend, Richard Johnson . . . Dick Johnson. Making out in the back seat of Dick's rust-colored Chevy Chevelle with vinyl interior was an important summer pastime.

I didn't have time for a job.

But I was going to have to get a job . . . if I wanted to go to Summer Jam. My parents were digging in. My mom wanted me to work at Dillon's grocery store. My dad wanted me to work at his law office. But I was still hanging on to my summer plans of getting drunk with my friends and getting a tan.

Then it hit me . . . Four years earlier we put a swimming pool in our backyard. In case you don't know, Kansas is nothing like California. A backyard pool is a terrible idea. It's snowing, raining, lightning, or a tornado is coming 320 days a year.

So my summer job . . . I was going to give swimming lessons in my backyard.

I hadn't taken lifeguarding nor given a lesson on any subject, but I was on the swim team.

Half a dozen students signed up.

Eight-year-old Wade Chung was one of my students. His family had just moved to Kansas from Korea. One day Mrs. Chung asked, "Do you know anyone who could teach Wade French?"

"Well yes I do. I can teach Wade French."

I taught Wade everything I knew: We counted to ten. I taught him the words for cat, dog, months of the year . . . not in order. I taught Wade six days of the week.

My summer job was muy bien . . . I had money for Summer Jam!

The big day arrived. One hundred and eighty miles to Kansas City.

Afternoon: Triumph, Loverboy.

Evening: John Cougar, and then the band we had waited for our entire teenage lives . . . REO SPEEDWAGON about to take the stage . . . when the music stops, lightning crashes, thunder rolls, the sky turns from blue to black, the air grows still, tornado sirens blare, heavy rain falls—and the PA instructs us to follow the signs to the nearest tornado shelter.

Where we sit for the REST OF THE NIGHT.

"This is *merde*," I said.

That means shit in French.

Wade knows that word, too.

Andi Rosenthal

Andi Rosenthal received a BA degree in English from the University of Delaware and a dual MA in medieval literature and creative writing from Temple University. Andi's first novel, *The Bookseller's Sonnets*, published by Roundfire Books in 2010, was selected as a National Jewish Book Council "Book of Note" in 2012 and a Hadassah-Brandeis Institute "Conversations" book club selection. Andi is a contributing writer to *eJewish Philanthropy*, Reform Judaism, Kveller, and InterfaithFamily. She is a frequent lecturer on the subject of synagogue engagement, outreach, conversion, and interfaith issues. Andi is an accomplished musician, and in addition to playing seven instruments, she also sings with a number of local choirs. She is a native of Westchester County and lives in New Rochelle, New York.

Driver's Seat

Andi Rosenthal

You sit in your Oldsmobile Cutlass Supreme, hands clenched white on the wheel; it is the final hour that separates July from August of 1987. You are seventeen years old, hazel eyed, with auburn hair cut asymmetrically. In front of you, just beyond the windshield, lie the waters of a lake called Innisfree, named for the Yeats poem you studied this past year as a junior in Honors English. The lyric chants itself as you feel the car's soft upholstery through your torn white shorts: "I shall arise and go now, and go to Innisfree." But it is not the Irish lake that Yeats loved which looms in front of you. It is instead a small, deep local pond approximately four minutes from the suburban New York home where you grew up, and you are parked there, deciding whether to drive headlong into it.

You take your hand from the wheel and run it over the pillowy front seat, wondering how quickly the water will fill the wells of the driver and passenger sides, whether your body will float or sink, if there is some way to make the time between submerging and drowning pass more quickly. Your car is heavy and solid; you imagine it sunken like treasure among the creeping vines and soft sand of the underwater. You think of Chappaquiddick, and how the divers found the girl with her pale, pretty face pushed up against the rear window. You are not a delicate blonde, but a man and his desires have left you here at the water's edge, just the same.

For within the hour that has just passed, you somehow got up and walked out of the tiny basement bedroom, unlocking the door your boyfriend had fastened shut. The entire party was reduced to the beat of the music and the strength of his body as he pushed you down, held your wrists and forced your clothes off. Afterward, you somehow managed to pull yourself together; you tolerated his apology and stumbled to your car. You drove to the other side of the lake, to the beach where he first kissed you a year ago, when you were still a virgin and he was just a boy you knew from the next town over. You dimmed your headlights and considered your two options: Live with this truth, or die because of it.

Across the lake, the party continues into the night. You feel as if you are saying goodbye to your friends, to the world, as if within the flickering lights across the water, bright souls beam back messages of farewell. Your tentative foot feels for the gas pedal. A trembling hand lifts itself toward the gearshift, threatening to pull it down toward Drive.

You listen one last time to the outside world, windows open to the humid night, expecting the spattering of sand and gravel kicking out from under your wheels. You hear the lapping of water against the shoreline, and in that sound you understand you will have to carry this night in your heart forever, your chest full of sharp stones that will cut from the inside. You aren't sure you can live with this memory, now woven into every fiber of your torn clothes, the stain of blood soaking into the pale blue upholstery. You know that the water will wash away all these secrets, leaving this night to steel and silence.

With your hand on the gearshift, you look out through the windshield. The darkness is suddenly full of stars. A thin song emerges from the radio, harmonizes with the night sounds of water and wind. A moment passes; you flick on the headlights, put your foot to the pedal. You feel the heavy car push itself into reverse, and the stars blaze above as July becomes August. I shall arise and go, you tell yourself. You drive away.

Jim Russek

Producer **Jim Russek** created advertising and built memorable entertainment brands that have played to generations of audiences. He helped launch *A Chorus Line* on Broadway, led the ad campaign for Francis Ford Coppola's national tour of *Napoleon*, launched the *Big Apple Circus* at Lincoln Center and a phenomenon called Stomp, and created decades of award-winning work for Lincoln Center Theater. Away from work, Jim is part news junkie and part avid baseball fan. He conceived and produced the critically acclaimed musical revue *Bush Wars*. He also partnered with Bill "Spaceman" Lee to create a barnstorming team of former Boston Red Sox players, The New England Grey Sox.

A Giant Step Up

Jim Russek

The Stage Deli smelled like the hallway in my grandmother's Brooklyn apartment house—chicken soup with undertones of garlic and overtones of celery and dill. "Two corned beef on rye," I shout, "one with mustard; a tongue sandwich on rye, trim the *shlung* and if you don't, I'm back again in fifteen minutes and I want my tip back."

Oh, the food was not for me. I was the studio production assistant on *The Ed Sullivan Show*—the coffee boy. The previous season I was backstage as a CBS Page answering phones, looking around the studio for so-and-so's agent, and once helping pull the Rolling Stones in through the front door of Studio 50 to avoid the mob at the stage door around the corner.

But now, I was in a suit and tie schlepping to the Stage Deli for the producer and the director's lunch. A giant step up.

A few shows into the '67 season, the cue card guy was elevated to full-time production assistant. And I was next in line for the job. A job I would keep for four seasons. I wrote down George Burns's act in a suite at the Plaza Hotel. I sat with Sid Caesar at the coffee shop next to the theater—he told me someday I'd be a producer.

I put Joan Rivers's routine on cards a dozen times. She gave me generous tips after every appearance and invited me to Downstairs at the Upstairs to see her club act. And at the end of my first season, she thanked me with a weighty, solid silver pen.

And then there was the time Lainie Kazan sang Joni Mitchell's "Both Sides Now." A song way out of this great jazz singer's repertoire. A song whose lyrics do not repeat. She needed cue cards. And she needed glasses. Which meant the letters on the cue cards had to be four inches tall. Which meant there were ten stanzas of cloud's and love's and life's illusions in four-inch-high letters occupying dozens of cards.

Cue cards are written on twenty-two-inch by twenty-eight-inch poster board. You punch two holes at the top and use loose-leaf rings to hold them together so you can flip them. I would write in all capital letters with a liquid-ink magic marker—the fumes from which could get you high as an elephant's eye.

The lyrics for "Both Sides Now" must have weighed one hundred pounds.

And of course, Lainie was not going to stand frozen. The choreographer had her traveling all over the stage. I had to know which of three cameras had the shot at any given moment so I wouldn't get in the picture as I followed Lainie around flipping cards.

Dress rehearsal went great. I learned where to position myself, but the cards were so heavy the binder rings were cutting through them. I tried putting reinforcements over the holes to repair the damage.

As the clock struck eight on Sunday night, The Ed Sullivan Show went live all across America. During the final commercial break, Ms. Kazan comes out to her mark as do I. Sixty seconds later Mr. Sullivan reads her intro from a teleprompter. Music starts and here we go . . .

Rows and flows of angel hair and ice cream castles in the air and the very first card tears through the binder rings as I flip it. Rather than juggle, I toss the card into the snake pit of cables behind the center camera. Now I'm ducking under camera lenses to keep in front of Lainie. I'm reading lyrics upside down to know when to flip and ripping the cards off the rings once they're sung. By the end, cards are scattered everywhere. Lainie gets a huge ovation. I have sweat rings down to the pockets of my suit jacket. I am officially in show business.

Leanne Sowul

Leanne Sowul is an award-winning writer whose fiction and creative nonfiction credits include *Juxtaprose Magazine, Barnstorm Journal, Hippocampus Magazine,* and *Rappahannock Review*. An elementary school band teacher, she has directed more than two hundred student performances and can play every band instrument (just don't give her a cello). Her master's degree in humanistic and multicultural education led her to restorative social justice work, and she recently served on her school district's equity team and became one of the founding members of a local My Brother's Keeper chapter. Leanne lives with her husband, two young children, and cranky twenty-year-old cat in New York's Hudson River Valley.

The Band Room

Leanne Sowul

The low rumble of timpani mallets contrasts with the peaked pitch of teenaged voices as I enter the band room on the first day of high school. Shiny instruments emerge from cases big and small. Four half circles of chairs and music stands face a podium, and there's a folder with my name on it in the front row. I unpack my flute on my knees and blow a few soft, experimental notes across the mouthpiece while keeping my chin down to hide the fresh scar on my throat.

Six weeks ago, a surgeon slit my throat and scooped out my thyroid gland to remove the malignant tumor wrapped around it. There's still more cancer inside my lymph nodes. As my life split itself into before and after, I found myself focusing on one thing that still mattered to me: starting marching band before my freshman year. But band camp—required for learning routines to that year's show—was scheduled during my first week of cancer treatment. Instead of marching the field in patterns coordinated to the music I'd already memorized, slopping through mud and heat with my bandmates and giggling in bunk beds at night, I ingested radioactive iodine and spent four days isolated in a hospital room.

Today is the first time I've opened my flute case in weeks. Though the marching band director said I could play the show's music from the sidelines this season—a compromise for missing band camp—I'd said no. If I'd been given special circumstances, the whole marching band would find out why and I'd become the "cancer kid." Pity equals attention; I don't want either. If I try hard enough, maybe I can pretend the cancer doesn't exist here. Two separate worlds: one for cancer, one for school.

The wind ensemble director, Mr. Janove, raps his baton on the conductor's stand in front of me. As talk dies down, he meets my wide-eyed gaze and awards me what I'll learn is a rare but genuine smile. He directs us to take a piece of music from our folders, then raises his baton. We breathe as one and release our first sound.

Layers of tones vibrate from woodwinds, brass, and percussion. We listen for balance and intonation, then adjust. The tones condense, purify. We listen and adjust again, all without words. The next chord comes, and the next, and soon my heartbeat aligns with the beat of the baton and my skin thrums in harmony with each pitch. My summer without music left me parched, and now I'm guzzling it down. A swell of trapped emotion fights its way out of my chest and into the air of my flute.

Slowly, cautiously, I straighten my spine. I lift my chin.

The cancer will stay with me throughout high school, but only here in the band room do I allow myself to open the doors between my two worlds. I share my deepest fears with my bandmates, not with words, but with breath and tongue and silvery tone. The flutes wail their grief with me in plaintive melody. Saxophones and clarinets sing consolation; trumpets and trombones blare brassy-bright hope. The snare drum raps a strengthening cadence. Through music, we forge my soul's resting place.

The following year on the marching band field, my feet march to the music; I'm no longer on the sidelines.

Years later, I rap my own baton on a conductor's stand and give my students a not-so-rare smile. We breathe as one and release our first sound. They pass the music between them, listening and blending, communicating their hearts through breath and tongue and silvery tone. Fears are shared, grievances aired, anxieties voiced. The band absorbs, diffuses, and transforms it all into melodious salve and harmonious joy.

I look out over the band room, watching my students. Slowly, cautiously, they straighten their spines. They lift their chins.

Angela Derecas Taylor

Angela Derecas Taylor was born and raised in 1960s Greenwich Village. She had a twenty-year career as chef, caterer, and event planner. Her next career, as executive assistant to the mayor of New Rochelle, lasted seventeen years. Now, in addition to writing creative nonfiction, Angela is an award-winning live storyteller, with performances on The Moth mainstage and on NPR on her resume. She is a certified yoga instructor and co-founder of Key to the Castle Workshop. Angela has been married for almost three decades to her husband, Tom. They are the proud parents of two adult sons and a rescue cat named Mario Plomo.

The Turkey Shoot

Angela Derecas Taylor

I was five years old, and it was the start of the holiday season. My parents separated when I was four months old. I'd never spent a single holiday with both of my parents, and the visitation agreement allowed for Dad to have me every other Sunday. Who would get me on holidays was left to my parents to work out on their own.

One Sunday, before Thanksgiving, Dad planned to bring me to a turkey shoot, an annual outing he attended in New Jersey with his sister, my Aunt Sophie, and her husband, Uncle Jim. Getting a bullseye meant winning a Thanksgiving turkey.

"She's too young," Mom said. "This is an adult thing."

"She'll be fine," Dad said. "Her Aunt Sophie will keep an eye on her."

"Last time you brought this kid back from Jersey, she had a broken arm and head lice!" Mom yelled. "Why can't you just take her to the park and get her an ice cream?"

I was the only child at the event, roaming freely among preoccupied adults. Adults with rifles. Shooting at targets.

All I cared about was winning a turkey. I was sure I could do it.

"Daddy, can I shoot?"

"No, you're too little."

I begged him. *Please. Let me shoot. I can do it. You're so mean! Let me shoot.* Please! I kept pestering until I wore him down. Finally, Dad lifted me onto a stool so that we stood, more or less, at the same height. With my back nestled against his chest, we extended our arms together along the cold steel barrel of the rifle. Dad raised the rifle to take aim, helping wrap my tiny forefinger and thumb around the trigger before placing his fingers on top, the rest of his big, strong hand enveloping mine.

My body tingled with anticipation. I knew we were going to win a turkey, and that would show Mommy how great Daddy was. Then maybe she'd let me go with him on Thanksgiving Day—and maybe stop saying all those mean things about him.

Dad and I were cheek to cheek as he nudged my head aside to look through the viewfinder. Then he allowed me to look, and I squeezed one eye closed like I'd watched him do, staring hard at the bullseye in the center of the target.

"Ready to win a turkey?" he asked.

"Yes, Daddy!"

I took a deep breath and held it as we squeezed the trigger.

BOOM!

The blast of the shotgun caused a powerful kickback and the gunstock nailed me right between the eyes. I screamed in shock and pain as blood from a deep gash flowed down my face and into my mouth. People yelled that my dad was an idiot for letting me shoot, and my Uncle Jim, who'd been a medic in the Korean War, took over triage.

"A butterfly's good for now," he said. "She probably needs a stitch to avoid a nasty scar. Let's get her to the emergency room."

"Nah," Dad said. "She'll be fine. But look at *this*!"

Dad held up the target paper showing the hole my bullet had made right at the very edge of the still-intact bullseye. "My best damn shot of the day."

I moved the ice pack away and raised my throbbing head, squinting through swelling eyelids at the paper target.

"Did we win the turkey, Daddy?"

"No. The *hump* wouldn't give it to us," Dad replied, disgusted. He held my chin and studied my face, turning it from side to side. "Hmm. Your mother's gonna *love* this."

"I'm sorry, Daddy," I blubbered, wiping the blood, tears, and snot with my sleeve.

That year, I spent Thanksgiving with my mom.

Julie Trelstad

Julie Trelstad is the director of Julie Ink Creative Author Consulting, an agency specializing in helping authors grow their online presence. An expert in book publishing, Julie has spent two decades on the frontlines of the digital publishing frontier. For most of her career, Julie was an acquisitions editor for homebuilding, architecture, and construction books, working at various publishers, including *Reader's Digest, the Taunton Press,* and *John Wiley & Sons*. She's best known for acquiring the book *The Not So Big House* by Sarah Susanka. Julie founded the Plain White Press, a nonfiction publishing company based in White Plains, New York, which she sold to Fox Chapel Publishing. Before founding Julie Ink, Julie spent several years at Writers House, a literary agency where she managed the agency's digital publishing program. When she's not dancing or helping authors, Julie is currently finishing her first novel.

The Salsa Lesson

Julie Trelstad

"One little detail," says Carlos as he walks me back to the middle of the dance studio floor. He poses my fingers—pinky up, middle fingers slightly dipped, the delicate inside of my elbow exposed. I count. There are at least ten little details.

My parents dressed up to go to country club balls. Kansas in the 1970s was a different time and a different place, but I thought that was what married people did. Marrying a guy who made extravagant excuses not to be led out onto the floor—usually "I'm hungry," or "I just ate"—was one of the disappointments of my adult life.

Carlos leaves me to practice alone. Fluttering with self-consciousness, I move my arm in and out like a baby bird—shoulder, elbow, wrist, fingers—while Carlos corrects my husband's hand signals.

My husband, Graham, looks confused. "I can't get her to do what I want her to do. Sometimes she just stands there."

Carlos smiles. "When we pull too hard, the women spin too soon. Too soft, they make things up."

Graham listens, nods. A wide smile breaks his face. "Who's in control? I am!"

In the language of the dance studio, as in many other places, the men are *we*, and women are *they*. In the opposing sides of salsa, I seem to be on the wrong one. I want to be the one to lead. Why can't I spin when I want to?

We have been taking private salsa lessons for two years now. We began dancing at the same time we started couple's therapy. I was prepared to walk out on my marriage if I was going to spend the rest of my life with a man who wouldn't dance with me.

Dancing was only one item in a list of grievances. Our life together had become cramped and uncomfortable since our twins had left the nest. In therapy we sat still on a couch tracing the patterns that we'd worn into the floor of our marriage, the ones we'd repeated so many times that we had come in danger of falling through.

Carlos can see that we're getting frustrated. He leads us over to the stereo cabinet and offers us a sip of *cafecito*. As we caffeinate, shake off our morning fog, Carlos says, "Grab my arm." Like a boy on a playground showing his muscles, he tenses so hard that moving it is like lifting a heavy weight. "That's what you're doing to him," he says to me. "Relax."

"Yes!" says Graham, as if letting go were something I could easily do in a situation involving three-inch heels and ever-more-complicated choreography.

My heels snap on the wood as we return for another round. Graham is noiseless in his plain black Capezios.

In the first months of our lessons, I refused to look Graham in the eye. I blamed it on being too busy trying to get my feet to do the foreign steps, but mostly I was surprised that I wanted to run away as much as I wanted to learn to dance.

Our therapist taught us that there are three of us in the relationship—me, him, and the couple.

Our couple makes the dance. In the dance, we're not equals, we're both necessary halves. He leads. I follow. Our steps fall into sync. I'm learning to be okay with that, even if it contradicts my sense of myself as a modern woman.

Graham spins me. I feel weightless. Carlos stops us. "One more little detail."

Frances Tunno

Fran Tunno is a copywriter, blogger, and voice actress. It's the kind of multitasking career that kept her in the game during the many years she lived in Los Angeles. You may have heard her on any one of the thousands of ads she's done, or for those who prefer something a bit more noncommercial, Fran has also voiced many audiobooks. Her blog won a BlogHer Voices of the Year Award, and she has published essays in the *LA Times, Pittsburgh Post-Gazette, La Gazetta Italiana*, and on various websites. Fran is also a maniacal baker, cook, and former morning radio personality. She survived mothering three children, who seem surprisingly well adjusted. Fran moved back to Pittsburgh to be closer to her Italian family and, of course, for the food.

The Power of Love and Pizza

Frances Tunno

When I was a teenager in the 1970s, the combination of my mom's thick Italian accent, lack of education, 1940s hairstyle, booming voice, and obesity made me cringe when my friends were around. So, Mother-Daughter Night, sponsored by the Girls Athletic Association, was an event I did not want my mom to attend.

I said something snotty like: "Oh girls and their moms will be in the gym. They'll be running around in shorts, playing volleyball and basketball. I don't know what you'd do there, but you can come if you want."

She couldn't hide the disappointment in her voice. "You don't a want a me dare. I'll a look a like a big a buffalo wit all a dose a skinny mothers." With resignation and attempted cheer, she said, "It's a okay honey, you go without a me. Have a good a time a."

A good daughter would have felt terrible, but I was relieved. I knew she wouldn't be able to play like the other mothers. And I didn't want everyone knowing my mom was more like everyone else's grandmother. Plus, she was always telling people how wonderful I was, and I was afraid people would laugh at us.

So, my mom stayed home and I went to GAA night with my best friend Carolyn, her young, thin mother, and a little something my mom sent.

All night, I watched mothers in blue jeans and shorts doing acrobatic leaps as they played volleyball. While I played, my self-absorbed, teenage brain kept thinking, *Why can't my mother be cool like this?* Why did she have to wait until she was forty-two to have me? Why does she have to be overweight, and why does she still have that dumb accent? I felt low and alone all night. Then it was time to eat.

My mom knew she wasn't coming, so the little something she sent was two pizzas the size of large cookie sheets. She'd baked them the day before, and they became her ambassadors.

After we played, we settled in the gym bleachers for snacks. I brought out the pizzas my mother had carefully wrapped in aluminum foil. I checked them for weird ingredients because occasionally I'd come home, smell something good and garlicky, open the oven door, and recoil at the sight of a split head of a goat sizzling away. Since Mom never wasted anything, I had to make sure she hadn't slipped any goat-y surprises into a pizza.

After they checked out, I sliced them, passed them around, and waited, hoping people liked them. Things were quiet, then I heard whispers. Mothers, daughters, and even the gym teacher started asking about the pizza . . . who brought it, who made it, and where could they get more? Everyone was raving about it, telling me how lucky I was. They said none of them ever got delicious homemade pizza like this.

In minutes, my mother became the most famous mother in GAA history who'd never touched a volleyball. With the *oohhhs* and *aaahhhs* echoing through the gym, you'd have thought these people had never tasted pizza.

I went from feeling like a pathetic orphan to the luckiest teenager in New Brighton. And the pizza wasn't even hot. It was cold, day-old pizza.

Later that night I sat alone in the bleachers staring at the brightly lit gym floor and felt ashamed. I felt guilty for all the times I'd wished my mom had been someone else, someone cooler, normal and American, who didn't roast goat heads.

Then, I made a vow: I'll never resent my mother for who she is and what she doesn't do. She does something just as important as the "normal" moms; she's simply in a different talent category.

When I got home, I thanked her and told her how much everyone loved her pizza and how lucky they said I was. I'll never forget her smile.

John Van Kirk

John Van Kirk is professor emeritus of English at Marshall University, where he taught literature and writing for twenty-three years. A navy veteran, he served as a helicopter pilot during the 1980s. He has sailed among the Greek islands and crossed the Atlantic in a thirty-eight-foot cutter. An O. Henry Prize winner, he is the author of *Song for Chance*, a novel, and numerous essays and short stories, and he recently completed a novel based on his experiences in the navy. He and his wife, Karen, are enjoying their retirement in Ashland, Kentucky. And he never misses the annual fly-fishing trip with his brothers, nephews, and, so far, one niece.

Under the Rain Fly

John Van Kirk

From the time of her diagnosis, it took our mother about a year and a half to die. Six months after the funeral, I drove the six hours to Carlisle, Pennsylvania, to meet my brothers and nephews for our annual fishing trip. It rained on and off as I crossed the West Virginia mountains, and I fished the Yellow Breeches Creek in gray light for a couple of hours before heading for the campground. My brothers would be driving in from New Jersey, and I didn't expect them until dark. I set up my small tent and a rain fly in a light drizzle, built a fire, and sat in a camp chair to await their arrival. By the time they got there—Cris and his two boys, Tyler and Patrick, in one car and Jeff and his son, Kyle, in another—the rain was pouring down.

It was the first time we'd all been together since the funeral, but we didn't talk about that. Back when we'd planned the trip, Cris had volunteered to make dinner the first night, so the rest of us went to work putting up the other tents while he set up shop on the picnic table under the rain fly, assembling the Coleman stove and firing up the lantern.

"Have you seen Dad lately?" I asked. "How's he doing?"

"He's all right. Lonely," Jeff said, as he put the tent poles together.

"Yeah."

Gradually, the tents carved out their bits of dry air from the wet. Under the fly, steam was rising from the pots on the stove.

"So what's for dinner, Cris?"

"It's a surprise," Cris said.

That was fine. We are not a family that believes camping is an excuse for primitive food. Even when we have steaks with potato salad, the potato salad is homemade, according to our mother's recipe, and if you want to see a superior sneer, just put a plastic container of store-bought macaroni salad in front of one of us. Traditional camping trip meals for us are chicken a la king, made from scratch with fresh mushrooms and freshly grilled chicken in the cream sauce; homemade chili over rice; spaghetti with sausage and meatballs. Even the sandwiches we eat for lunch are garnished with sun-dried tomatoes.

At last, it was time. Cris opened the smaller of the pots and ladled rice into plastic bowls. Then he took the lid off the larger pot. The aroma hit me like a summer wind, cutting through the damp and the seething rain with the warmth of being kissed goodnight by your mother.

"Is that what I think it is?" Jeff said.

"What?" Kyle said.

"Lamb curry," I said. "Mom used to make it. I haven't had it in probably ten years. Where'd you find a recipe?"

"It's Mom's recipe," Cris said. "Found it in one of her old cookbooks."

"Did you bring chutney?" I asked.

"What do you think?" Cris said. "It wouldn't be complete without the chutney."

The rain poured down around us. The next day we would fish between showers and come back later to find our campsite so thoroughly drenched that we would break camp and leave a day early. But right then we sat and savored the rich flavors of a dish our mother made when we were boys, the sweet spicy tang of the mango chutney, the tender lamb sharp with curry, the bright green peas, the bits of apple, the sauce turning the perfect rice yellow under the light of the lantern. We looked at one another as we ate. A spectacular meal in its own right, it was also a memory of meals we had taken to be ordinary, but that memory was made extraordinary now that the woman who prepared them for us was gone. We still weren't talking about our mother, but we knew that as the evening went on we would.

Sarah Bracey White

Sarah Bracey White and her husband live in Ossining, New York, but in her heart and through her pen she is a Southern storyteller, mining her life for poems, essays, and stories. In 2021 her memoir, *Primary Lessons*, transformed into an immersive, dramatic musical and debuted as a live performance at the Paramount Theater in Peekskill, with Sarah in the starring role. Other literary work includes *The Wanderlust: A South Carolina Folk Tale* and *Feelings Brought to Surface*, a poetry collection. Her work has been collected in several anthologies and has also appeared in *The New York Times, the Baltimore Afro-American Newspaper, The Scarsdale Inquirer,* and *the Journal News.*

Camp Cook

Sarah Bracey White

In 1963, days after my graduation from a segregated South Carolina high school, I boarded a train for Ely, Vermont, where, even though I knew little about cooking, I was to be the head cook's assistant at an exclusive girls' camp nestled on the shores of Lake Fairlee. I dreamed of learning to swim in the beautiful lake pictured in the camp's brochure. Upon arrival, however, Camp Beenadeewin's owner told us that the kitchen help was not allowed to go near Lake Fairlee. We also were told not to associate with the white campers and to address each one as Miss during all encounters in the dining hall. Up north, it seemed segregation was a matter of class and skin color.

I was incensed and wanted to bolt, but I had no way to get home, and no home to return to. My mother had died a few months earlier, and I'd had no contact with my absentee father for years. Beenadeewin was to have been my interim home until I entered Morgan State College that fall. The camp's offer of room, board, a roundtrip train ticket, and three hundred dollars in exchange for two months' labor no longer seemed fair, but I accepted my fate.

Mrs. Lee, the head cook, six other teenaged girls, and I quickly settled into the routine of preparing and serving home-cooked meals for 150 people three times a day, six and a half days a week. It was cold and dark each morning as I made my way through the pine-scented forest to the kitchen, where I stirred huge vats of Maypo, loaded slices of white bread onto an industrial-sized toaster, then buttered and pressed each slice into a plate of cinnamon sugar. Under Mrs. Lee's tutelage, I learned to make, and enjoy, delicacies like sugar cookies, cloverleaf dinner rolls, and smooth, brown gravy for pot roasts.

Despite my anger about the restrictions at camp, I was shamelessly curious about the campers. Never before had I been in such close proximity to so many white people my age. From my side of the kitchen counter, it grew easier day by day to eavesdrop on their conversations as they grew used to our brown presence and we became about as insignificant as the pine trees.

I soon learned that white skin brought no solace from money problems and didn't ensure smooth boy-girl relationships or prevent sadness and heartache. They had the same problems I had! I also learned that having two parents at home didn't always make a happy family.

Every Sunday afternoon, the resident handyman took the seven of us sightseeing in the camp's old, woody station wagon. I marveled at the beauty of the Vermont countryside and the quaintness of its villages. I surmised from the stares that our little group always drew that no other colored people had ever lived in, or visited, the state of Vermont. An overwhelming sense of being different, and unwelcome, permeated my entire experience.

The last Sunday afternoon before camp ended, instead of joining the weekly tour, I made a pilgrimage through the pine forests to the forbidden Lake Fairlee. As I looked out over the vast, mirror-like expanse, I grew angry. What right did white people have to bar me from something God made? Since they thought my skin would contaminate their lake, I decided to do something that really would. I stepped into the water, squatted, and peed.

Rhonda Zangwill

Rhonda Zangwill has long flirted with the literary life, writing, editing, teaching, and rabble-rousing for New York Writers Coalition, *Writers Read*, PEN Prison Program, and The Moth. She now runs writing workshops for the Educational Alliance and Sirovich Senior Center. Her published work, both print and online, can be found in *Calyx, Natural Bridge, Hoi Polloi, The Boston Globe*, and, most recently, the 2024 *National and International Goddess Anthology*. Last year she was honored to have been nominated for a PushCart Prize. She reads around town, including at the National Arts Club, the NYC Poetry Festival, East Village Wordsmiths, and, thanks to Fahrenheit Open Mic, in some of the East Village's most charming community gardens.

Out on a Limb

Rhonda Zangwill

Long before 23andMe became a thing, I had my own ancestry hotline: my father's library. It was crowded with books by writer Israel Zangwill, the forebear my father claimed, as did his father before him. Maybe you know some titles: *Children of the Ghetto, The King of Schnorrers, The Melting Pot*. Yes, the very pot that all of us bubble in every day. Well, it was Israel Zangwill, a British Jew, who coined that phrase on an American literary tour in 1908. He took one look at our huddled masses and transformed us into an enduring metaphor.

What a claim to fame! And one that has, over the years, compelled complete strangers to squeal in delight upon learning my name: *Zangwill? Are you related to Israel?? I love him!* Once a postal clerk gave me a big grin and tapped his yarmulke before handing me my mail. And the socialist rabbi in Capetown? He nearly fainted when I introduced myself. For him, Israel Zangwill was no less than the "Jewish Dickens."

Wait, there's more. In 1923, Izzy (as I call him) was voted—I kid you not—"the third most outstanding Jew in the world." In the world! There was a contest. Compliments of The Jewish Times in Britain. They asked people to come up with a list of their top twelve Jews. Brilliant! Who doesn't love a list? Why twelve? Why not? Maybe they thought, *How about one for each of the twelve tribes of Israel?* Or, one for every month. Can you imagine the fundraising calendar? A whole year of outstanding Jews!

Then, something more amazing happened: On September 17, 1923, Izzy graced the cover of Time magazine. Not the number one Jew, Albert Einstein (who else?) or number two, Chaim Weitzman. But number three. Overnight, at least in America, Izzy's bronze medal was suddenly gold.

Let's be honest, isn't this one reason so many people search for their roots? To discover someone famous perched in the family tree? To revel in a genetic link to celebrity?

That said, my connection to Izzy is distant. Some kind of cousin, God only knows how many times removed. But distance only makes my heart grow fonder. I love that I share a bloodline with such a respected writer, wit, and—icing on the cake—feminist. Here's a guy who, in support of the female agitators of his day—1907—said, "we shall not rest until this barbarous handicap of sex is wiped out from the statute books of civilization."

I realize that family lore is not what genealogists consider cold hard evidence. For that I count on my brother, who has spent years digging up proof of our kinship with Izzy. He writes endless letters, researches every mention, connects even the faintest of dots.

But I have something my brother does not. I have copies of letters written by the man himself. And they reveal some tantalizing—possibly DNA-based—traits we share. For instance:

Izzy suffered from insomnia.

I have insomnia!

Izzy's close friend was Russian revolutionary Peter Kropotkin. Today forgotten, but not by me! I've schlepped my cherished copy of Kropotkin's memoirs with me everywhere for forty-five years.

Finally, Izzy was devoted to women's suffrage.

Not to brag, but I always vote. Every election. Even local.

Best, though, was whom Izzy was writing to: Emma Goldman! Anti-war radical, birth control pioneer, all-around rabble-rouser. I have claimed her as spiritual foremother since the '70s, inspired by her passion and courage and humor and, not least, the fact that J. Edgar Hoover called her "the most dangerous woman in America." My treasured Emma-Izzy correspondence is for me a kind of familial beacon, lighting my path.

So I don't need to spit in a test tube. I already have the third most outstanding Jew nestled up with the most dangerous woman. With these two in my corner, Ira Gershwin said it best: "Who could ask for anything more?"

Writers Read

Giving Voice to the Stories That Bind Us.

THE
LOFT
AT
writers READ
writersread.org

Reading
writers
READ

June 30, 2024 · 2:00 PM
The Linda Auditorium · Albany, NY

Afterword

Writers Read gives voice to the stories that bind us, and the collection you hold in your hands has been woven from the fabric of real lives—stories of joy, loss, love, surprise, and everything in between.

Selected from among the many hundreds of 5-minute, 650-word stories we've presented on the *Writers Read* stage during our first ten years, the true, personal tales I selected for this volume are among my favorites; I'm as proud to present them here as I was when I first heard them read aloud to attentive, appreciative audiences.

A celebration of both ordinary and extraordinary moments, these literary snapshots invite listeners—and readers—along for the ride, taking us inside the writer's experience. From a vicarious walk of the red carpet at the Academy Awards to a climb up the branches of a family tree, each one reflects the complexity, the humor, and the beauty of being human.

As you turn these pages, take a moment to reflect on your own truths. What events in your life have shaped you? And what stories would you tell, if given the chance?

Writers Read's mission is to create performance opportunities for writers, and I've had the pleasure and privilege of producing more than fifty live performances over the past decade. I've witnessed how storytelling—whether on a small stage, around a kitchen table, or on the pages of a book—has the power to heal, connect, and inspire. Some of these personal essays might remind you of moments in your own life, while others will introduce you to experiences you've never considered. As you explore and absorb and revisit these pages, I hope you find yourself reflected in the words, or at least moved by what each story represents.

If you're a writer, I encourage you to review the submission calls on our website to see if a current prompt inspires you. And please come to one of our events to experience the kind of magic that takes place as people lean in, focused and listening, when a writer tells his or her story.

Here's to the stories that have already been told—and to the many more still waiting to be shared.

—Edward McCann, *Writers Read* Founder

Congratulations!

You've stumbled upon the legendary QR Code of Donations—
a mystical portal to a realm of generosity and possibility.

Simply scan this enchanted code, and —voilà!—you'll be transported to a dimension where your kindness is transformed into magical resources supporting our mission to create performance opportunities for writers.

Please reach for your device, scan the code, and let your contribution open the gates to a world where every dollar is an investment that casts a spell of positive change.

Who knew doing good could be so much fun?

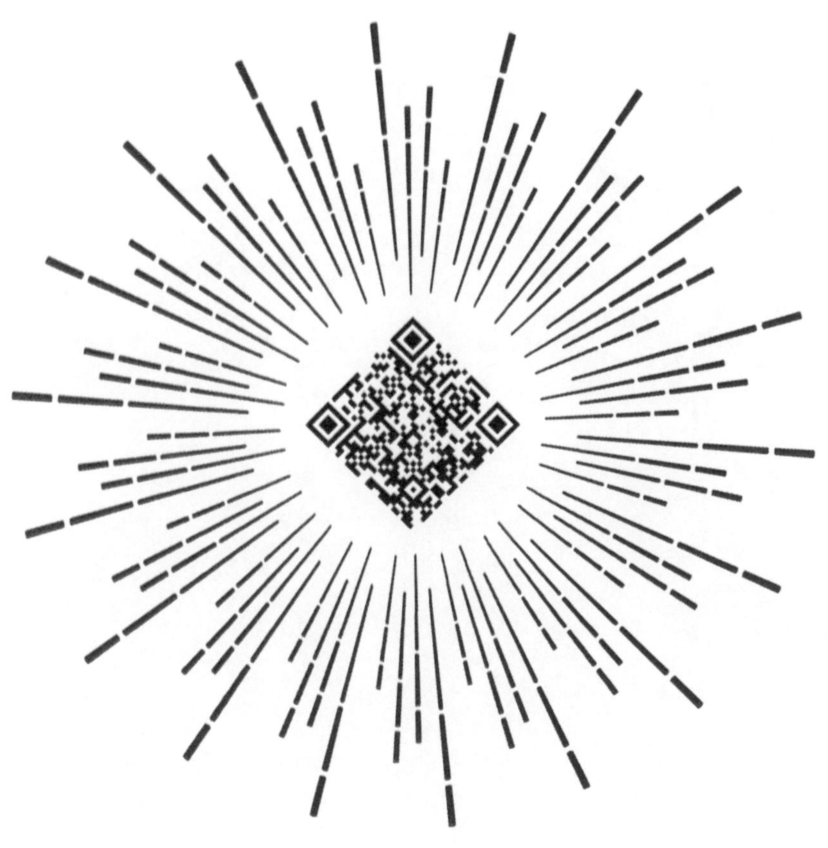

writers
READ™
writersread.org

www.ingramcontent.com/pod-product-compliance
Lightning Source LLC
Chambersburg PA
CBHW030607310726
48979CB00003B/603

* 9 7 8 1 7 3 4 3 8 0 8 6 6 *